Michael Caine

In Person

18 YEARS 59 DAYS

Michael Owen

In Person

CollinsWillow

An Imprint of HarperCollinsPublishers

First published in 2000 by CollinsWillow
an imprint of HarperCollins*Publishers*
London

1 3 5 7 9 8 6 4 2

A CIP catalogue record for this book is available from the British Library

ISBN 0 00 218937 2

Colour origination by Arneg Ltd

Photographic Acknowledgements
Allsport 28, 35, 40(br), 44, 51, 73, 75, 76, 78, 79, 82, 83, 85, 87, 101, 102, 105, 106,
108(t), 108(b), 109(t), 109(b), 110(t), 110(b), 111(t), 111(b), 112(t), 112(b), 113(t), 120,
121, 122. **Cheetham Bell** 11, 91(l), 91(r), 92. **Clive Brunskill/Allsport** 1, 12, 13, 39, 48, 90,
93, 118. **Marc Aspland/The Times** 40(bl). **Pepsi-Cola** 45, 88, 95, 97. **Reuters** 36, 40(t).
Simon Fowler 18, 25. **Umbro International** 41, 47, 54, 58, 59, 65, 94, 116. **Walkers** 38,
50, 114. All other photographs supplied courtesy of SFX Entertainment.

Printed and bound in Great Britain by Scotprint Ltd, Mussselburgh

The HarperCollins website address is:
www.**fire**and**water**.com

Contents

> *'When it came to choosing my commitment to one particular nation as a footballer, it was no contest. I am an Englishman through and through.'*

BEGINNINGS

At various times when I was growing up as a football-crazy kid, it was difficult to know whether I was English, Welsh or Scottish. If that sounds confusing, let me try to explain. I was born in England – at a hospital in Chester – the fourth of five Owen children, and to be quite honest I have never felt anything other than an Englishman.

My dad Terry, a former professional footballer who played for Everton, Bradford City, Chester, and Cambridge United, had a Scottish mother and in fact lived up north of the border for several years when he was young. Like anyone with Scottish blood running through their veins, he feels very patriotic towards them and loves to see their national teams excel at all sports – with the obvious exception of when they are playing against England at football.

Having entered the world on a maternity ward in Chester, I was brought up in the family home in Hawarden, a small town just over the Welsh border. I stayed there for 19 years until I had my own house built, barely a mile or so up the road. So it is an indisputable fact that I have lived all my life in Wales.

When it came to choosing my commitment to one particular nation as a footballer, it was no contest. I am an Englishman through and through. While I recognise my dad's tartan ancestry and the fact that I was raised and educated in Wales, it was always the roar of the three lions that stirred my patriotism. I do not mean to be disrespectful to the Welsh but I would say 80 per cent of the kids I went to school with believed they were English as well.

However, I did get close to playing for Wales as a schoolboy international. Because I attended Hawarden High School, I qualified to wear the red shirt of that country and attended a couple of trial sessions, when I was 13. Even though I had a chance of playing international football with boys two years older than me, I had to tell them I was not going to pledge my allegiance to them because I was determined to play for England.

' *My whole family grew up in a sporting environment and we thrived upon it.* '

At that stage of my football development I was quietly confident of winning a place at the Football Association's School of Excellence at Lilleshall which would more or less guarantee me a schoolboy cap for England. I did not want to jeopardise that possibility.

My life as a youngster was dominated by sport – especially football. I don't suppose I had much choice really because of my dad's career as a footballer but he never forced it upon me. My whole family grew up in a sporting environment and we thrived upon it.

My two older brothers Terry and Andrew were both keen footballers and the women in the family were very active on the sports field as well. My mum Janette used to do a lot of athletics when she was at school and I think all the kids inherited her natural speed as a runner. My older sister Karen ran and played hockey for the county teams and younger sister Lesley is an excellent netball player.

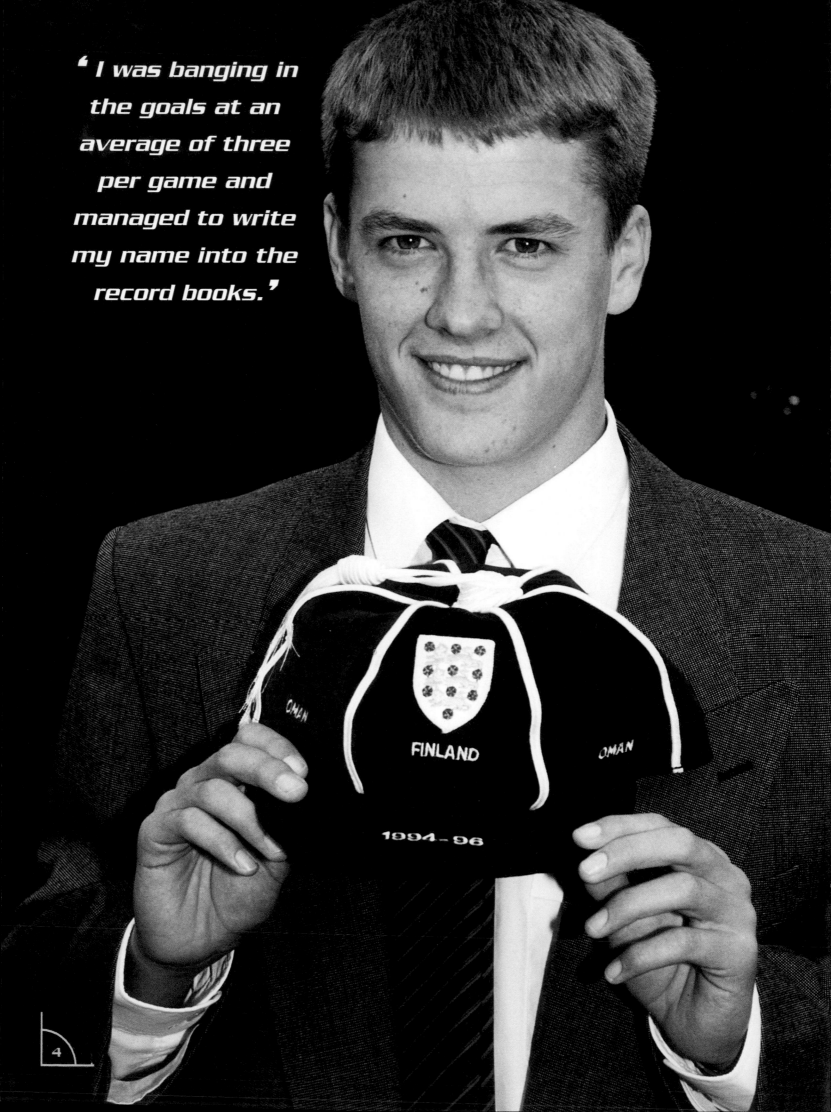

'I was banging in the goals at an average of three per game and managed to write my name into the record books.'

4

I loved everything about my upbringing. They reckon as soon as I could walk dad had me kicking a ball about in the back garden, and when I was old enough I would join him and my two brothers down the park for some highly competitive two-a-side matches. Apparently, even then I had a tremendous will-to-win and developed an early knack for scoring goals.

I was not all that big, in fact I was quite tiny for my age, but dad taught me the art of good timing when I kicked the ball and stressed the importance of being able to place the ball accurately past a goalkeeper rather than trying to blast the back of the net out.

Dad felt I was good enough to play proper organised football by the time I had reached the age of seven. He took me along to a local club side called Mold Alexander, some five miles away from where we lived, and asked the coaching staff whether they would consider me for one of their teams.

The youngest age group was the Under-10s and they were not too keen initially to let such a young lad join the team, but after a couple of training sessions they agreed to give me a go. I was named as a substitute at first. The team management did not want to leave out of the lads who had played for the club all season because it would have been unfair on them.

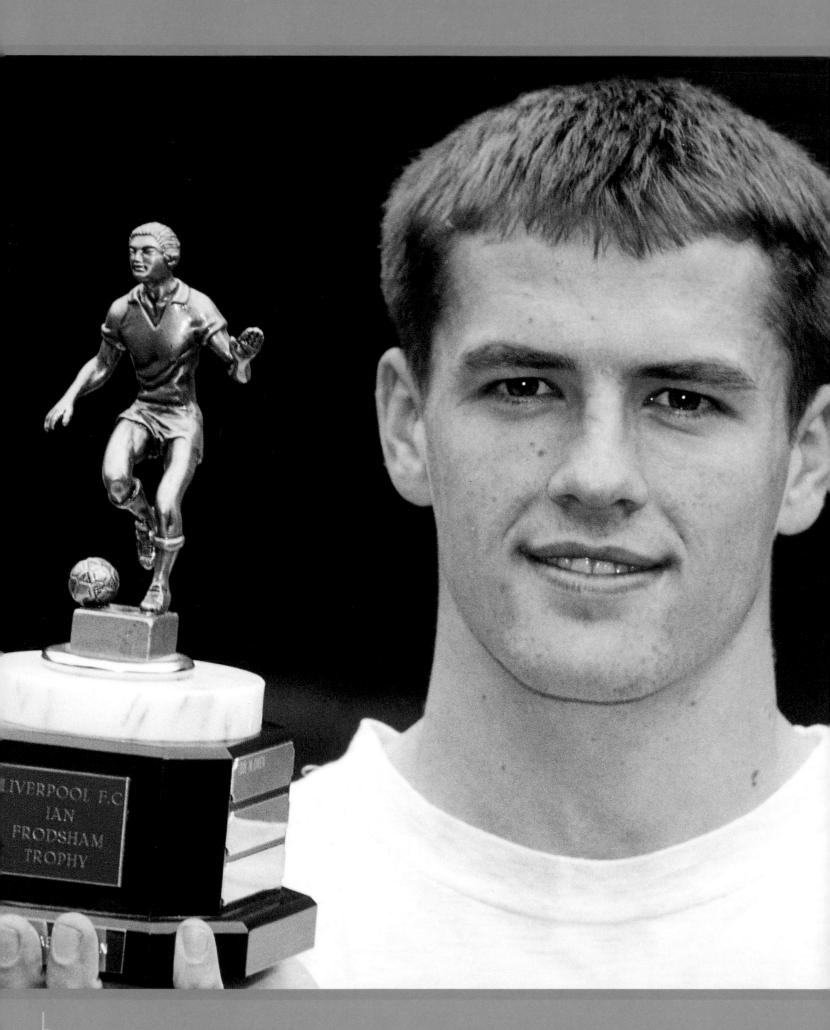

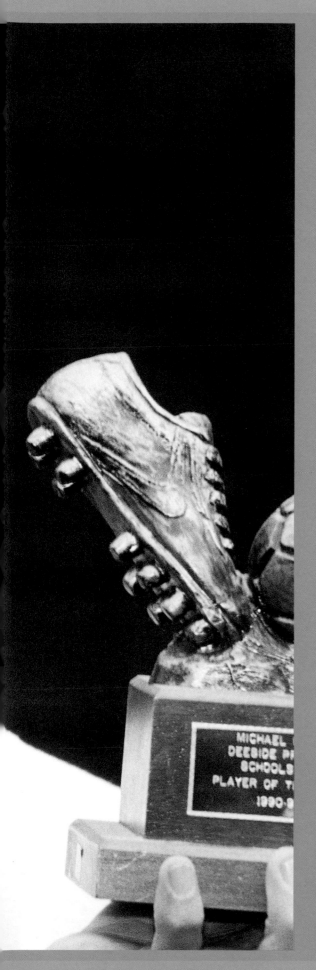

I was used for the last 20 minutes or so of each game and occasionally I would grab a goal or two in that time. Soon I became known as the club's secret weapon. All the time dad was giving me little tips and hints and teaching me good habits but was careful not to fill my head with too much tactical detail. He wanted me to just go out and enjoy myself and do what I was best at – scoring goals.

> *"I was keen on rugby and played at centre where I was able to use my running ability to score quite a few tries."*

At the age of eight I was picked for the Deeside Primary School side and I suppose that is when my ability as a footballer began to attract wider attention. I was banging in the goals at an average of three per game and managed to write my name into the record books. In one season I beat the goals total achieved by the legendary Liverpool striker Ian Rush.

Ian's best was 72 and I overtook that in exactly the same number of games. I went on to finish that season with 97 and soon word spread around the game that there was a youngster in Wales who was worth looking at. Scouts from Liverpool, Everton, Manchester United, Wrexham and Sheffield Wednesday all came knocking at the Owen door – but went away disappointed.

'My best time for 100 metres was 11.4 seconds which did not put me in the Linford Christie class but showed I was no slouch either.'

There was a strict rule laid down by the Deeside schools FA that professional clubs could not sign any of their players. I was not too concerned. I knew that if I continued to score goals and kept on improving, they would be back for another look.

After moving up to Harwarden High, I was offered the chance to visit many of the top professional clubs such as Manchester United, Everton, Tottenham, Arsenal and Chelsea. Eventually I chose to sign schoolboy forms with Liverpool. I was impressed with the friendly, homely atmosphere of the place.

I had grown up as a real Everton fan. My dad's influence obviously came into play there because he was able to get free tickets as one of their former players and he would often take the whole family along to Goodison Park to watch matches. So it must have seemed odd to some people for me to join Liverpool, but I was made really welcome by the youth development officer Steve Heighway and his staff. Free boots, playing kit and match-day tickets were always in plentiful supply and that helped to make me feel wanted at Anfield.

Once at high school, I became to expand my range of sporting activities. I was selected for the rugby, cricket and athletics teams and loved the competitiveness involved. I was keen on rugby and played at centre where I was able to use my running ability to score quite a few tries.

In the summer months I developed a great love for playing cricket. Most of our school matches were just friendlies against neighbouring schools, but I joined Hawarden Cricket Club and became captain of the Under-16 team. I opened the batting and bowling and in one match I was awarded a certificate signed by the former England captain Alec Stewart for scoring 92 runs. It remained my best ever total – and I claim to this day that the lbw decision given against me was highly dubious!

On the running track I excelled at sprinting. Anything further than 200 metres and you could count me out. I was still pretty small at 13 and 14 and while I was virtually unbeatable over 30 or 40 metres, the bigger lads were sometimes able to gallop past me in the closing stages of the 100 metres races. My best time for 100 metres was 11.4 seconds which did not put me in the Linford Christie class but showed I was no slouch either.

When I was 14, the thought of going to the School of Excellence at Lilleshall began to become more of a reality. It appealed to me because firstly it would prove I was among the top 16 schoolboy footballers in the whole country. It also meant I would probably win my first England cap as a schoolboy and give me a thorough grounding towards my ambition of becoming a professional footballer.

Liverpool had recommended me to the Football Association as a candidate for Lilleshall but I still had to go through a selection procedure along with hundreds of other boys from around the country. The first stage of the process was a little bit odd. I had to attend trials at Chester City's Deva Stadium where about 100 lads took part in four 20-minute match sessions.

The conditions were impossible. There was such a gale blowing it was impossible to string any sort of moves together. Whenever you tried to pass the ball the wind just took it hopelessly off course and I don't think a single trialist was able to show his true ability. I know I came away thinking I had done absolutely nothing to convince the selectors I was worth a place among the elite of England's schoolboy footballers.

' I was not alone during the initial couple of weeks in feeling homesick and even shed a tear or two as I struggled to adjust to a new way of life. '

Fortunately, they must have gone on past reputations. I had already started to make a bit of a name for myself as a Liverpool schoolboy and I was invited to attended further trials before finally being named among the 16 who had won a place at Lilleshall. It was a great honour but about a week before I was due to start it suddenly dawned on me that I was about to leave home at the tender age of 14.

I would have to leave all my family and friends behind and for two years devote my life to playing and training alongside the best young players in the country – as well as furthering my education in the classroom. I was not alone during the initial couple of weeks in feeling homesick and even shed a tear or two as I struggled to adjust to a new way of life.

We were all in the same boat, however, and I was more fortunate than most because my mum and dad only lived about an hour up the road from Lilleshall and were able to come and visit me each weekend. Gradually, we all got used to the lifestyle and thoroughly enjoyed ourselves though it was a pretty strict regime.

We lived in hostel-style accommodation under the care of Mr and Mrs Pickering. We would be woken at 6.45 every morning and had to be down for breakfast at 7.30, before catching the coach to the nearby Idsall High School where we joined the local pupils for our regular lessons.

We were known around the school as 'the footballers' but were not given any preferential treatment. It was also drummed into us from the outset that there should be no slacking as far as our schoolwork was concerned, even though most of us had high ambitions of becoming professional footballers rather than great academics.

I remember Mr Pickering telling us one day that out of the group of 16 only two of us could expect to make a good living in the game. I was so confident one of them was going to be me, I looked around the room and thought to myself: 'I wonder who the other one will be?' In the end, Mr. Pickering's assessment proved to be way off course. From my year Manchester United's Wes Brown, Everton's Michael Ball, Crewe's Kenny Lunt and Chelsea's Jon Harley all made it into the professional ranks.

My schoolwork inevitably took a back seat to football but I still managed to pass all 10 of my GCSEs with C and D grades. I know I could have done better if I had applied myself more thoroughly but by then I was pretty sure I was going to become a footballer and had been given a strong indication that Liverpool were going to sign me on trainee forms.

My academic qualifications might not have been so great but I benefited enormously from the football tuition. After school was finished we would spend two hours each evening out on the training ground and weekends were taken up with competitive matches. I made my debut for the England Under-15 and Under-16 teams and scored on both occasions.

I felt proud and honoured to receive my international cap from former England international Jimmy Armfield at the graduation ceremony which signalled the end of the two year course. Now I was ready to enter the football world with Liverpool.

"My academic qualifications might not have been so great but I benefited enormously from the football tuition."

One-to-One

Where were you born?	Countess of Chester Hospital (formerly West Cheshire Hospital)
What was your first football team?	Hawarden Pathfinders Cubs at 7
Who was your hero as a child?	Gary Lineker
What was your favourite food?	Steak and Chips
What was your favourite toy?	A football
Who was your best mate at school?	Michael Jones
Who was you first PE teacher?	Mr Ledsham
What was your favourite subject (other than PE)?	Geography
How old were you when you got you first pair of football boots?	Seven
Who was your first girlfriend?	Louise Bonsall
Where you ever in trouble at school?	No
What career would you have chosen if you had not made it as a football?	A professional golfer

UMBRO

> **'On my visits to Anfield as a schoolboy recruit, I soon recognised what a magnificent club Liverpool were.'**

LIVERPOOL

Because I grew up as an Everton fan, it will seem strange to many people to see how comfortably I made the switch of loyalty to Liverpool. On Merseyside the rivalry between the two clubs is so fierce that you are either blue or red. The two contingents rarely change sides.

I managed to do so because I was determined to choose the best football opportunities available to me. On my visits to Anfield as a schoolboy recruit, I soon recognised what a magnificent club Liverpool were. They had blazed a trail through English and European football and set the standards for the rest of the country to follow.

But despite all their achievements they retained the kind of homely atmosphere which made it easy for youngsters like me to feel accepted and wanted. Nothing was too much trouble when it came to the provision of facilities for kids they wanted to attract on board the Liverpool bandwagon.

So when I finished my course at Lilleshall, it took me no time at all to decide which professional club I was going to join. They immediately offered me a YTS contract which is the apprenticeship you serve before becoming a full-time pro.

You often hear stories of days gone by when the young, budding footballer was little more than a lowly paid servant who spent more time doing chores such as sweeping the terraces and dressing rooms, scrubbing the baths and showers and cleaning the seniors' boots than improving his football ability.

It doesn't work like that any more. The top clubs have caretakers, cleaners and cooks to carry out those duties once assigned to the overworked apprentice. All I had to do occasionally was sweep out the boot room – a job which took no more than a couple of minutes.

My YTS period did not last long. Normally a trainee would serve two years. After five months on a weekly wage of £42.50, I was offered a three-year contract as a professional on my 17th birthday and it meant a giant leap forwards in my earning power. I was to be paid £400 a week in my first year, £500 in my second and £600 in my third with a £5,000 signing-on fee.. It was incredible money for someone of my age and suddenly I was able to afford things that were never previously available to me.

' There is nothing quite like waking up every morning and really looking forward to going to work. '

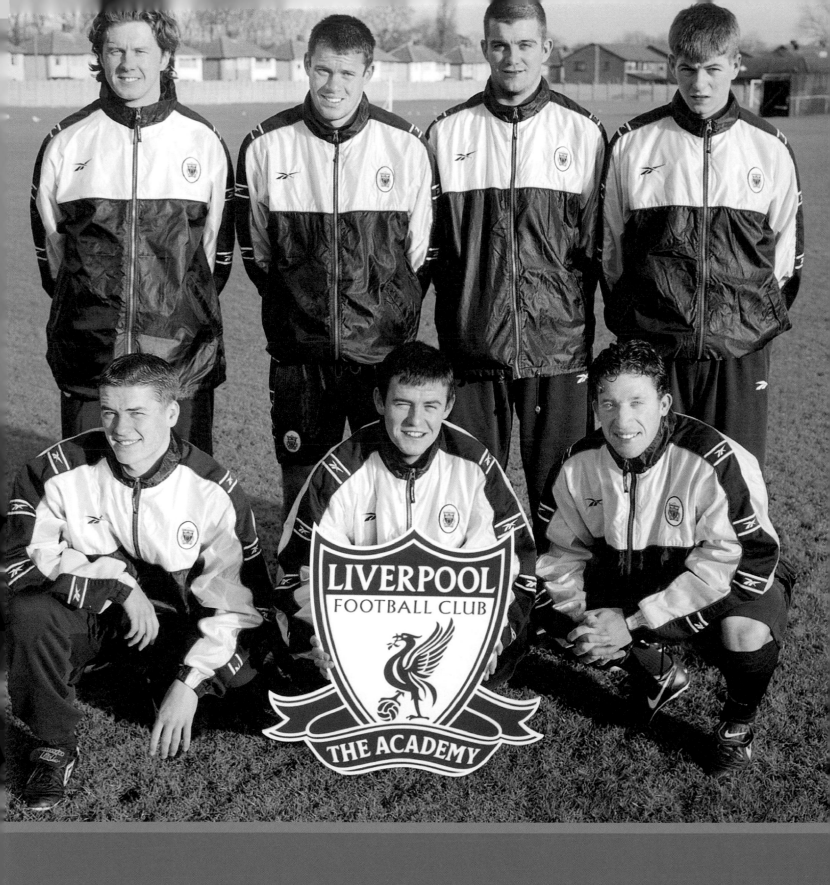

' He [Jamie Carragher] is a typical Scouser with a wicked sense of humour and takes the mickey out of anything and anyone.'

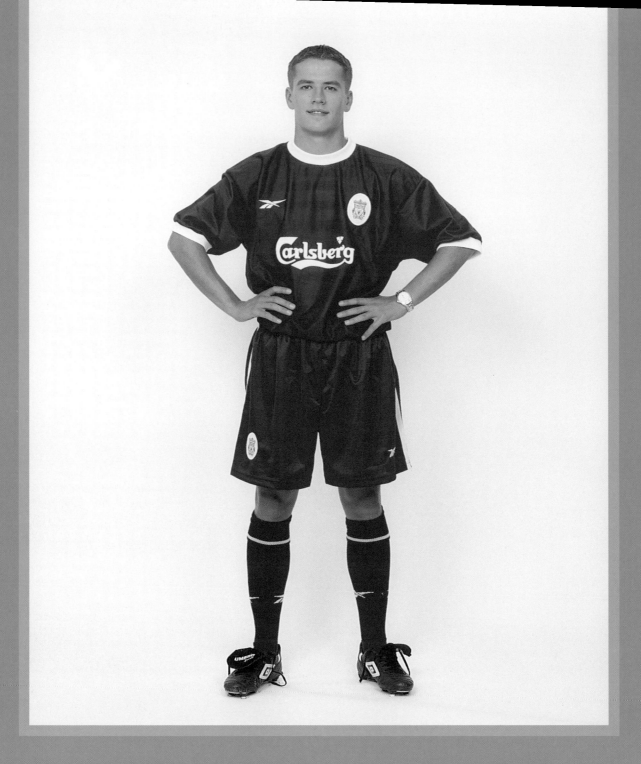

Not that I went on a massive spending spree – but I did splash out on a brand new car. When I first joined Liverpool my daily journey from home to the Melwood training ground took one and a half hours. I had to catch two trains and one bus each way. I could not wait to pass my test and my big day arrived when I was 17 years and four months old.

I remember returning home with my instructor after passing. I could see my dad cleaning his car on the drive. I was flashing my lights and giving him the thumbs up all the way down the road. We went straight to the local showroom and collected my brand new Rover Coupe at a cost of £18,000. We had already ordered it in advance of passing my test and it was a really proud moment for me to sit behind the wheel of my first car.

I did not go mad on any more luxuries after turning professional, though I did pay for me, mum and dad and my youngest sister Lesley to go on holiday to Spain.

'*I love the banter and humour which goes on around the football club. There is hardly a dull moment.*'

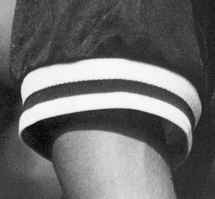

19

'I was offered a three-year contract as a professional on my 17th birthday and it meant a giant leap forwards in my earning power.'

Training with the Liverpool professionals was a great thrill for me and I soon developed a real love for my new life as a footballer. There is nothing quite like waking up every morning and really looking forward to going to work.

It can be hard work – especially before the season starts. Because of international duties, I only took part in my first pre-season before the 1999-2000 campaign. It was only then that I realised how much punishment the body can take. The club took us high up in the mountains in Switzerland and the twice daily sessions were a real slog.

My legs and feet were so battered that I used to lie on my hotel bed in the break between the two training stints and could hardly stir. But somehow I managed to drag myself to the afternoon sessions and push myself even further. I amazed myself at finding the extra stamina and willpower.

' I was on the bench a couple of times before actually kicking my first ball in the Premiership – and my first inclusion among the seniors caught me totally by surprise. '

But I have to admit that long-distance running is not my favourite pastime. When you are gasping for breath and your heart rate is up around the 200 mark it is not a great deal of fun, though I accept it has to be done to prepare you for the season ahead.

Once the season is underway the workload is less and training becomes more enjoyable – but still has to be taken seriously. We have to be in by 10 every morning for a 10.30 start and the sessions usually last for a couple of hours. Sometimes we have to stay on for an afternoon workout as well.

I love the banter and humour which goes on around the football club. There is hardly a dull moment. Even when you are travelling for three or four hours on a coach journey for an away game it never gets boring. We pass the time playing cards, watching videos and generally having a good laugh.

I am fortunate to have Jamie Carragher as my room-mate. He is a couple for years older than me but we broke into the Liverpool side at around the same time and have become really close pals. He is a typical Scouser with a wicked sense of humour and takes the mickey out of anything and anyone.

At the start of the 1999-2000 season, it was all-change in the Liverpool dressing room. It was a strange place to be at first with so many new faces, many of them foreign imports. There was Dutch goalkeeper Sander Westerveld, Swiss defender Stephane Henchoz, Finnish centre half Sami Hyypia, German midfielder Dietmar Hamann, Czech midfielder Vladimir Smicer, Guinean striker Titi Camara and Dutch forward Erik Meijer.

Most of them spoke more than a smattering of English so the language barrier did not really prove to be a problem. The one player in the squad who did struggle to communicate at first was our Cameroon defender Rigobert Song but he soon found a way to answer the dressing room mickey-takers who tried to wind him up. His first English words were all of the four-letter variety and he want not afraid to let rip with a few well-chosen swear words.

In addition to the overseas players, there was also a good selection of young local players making their way into the first team squad such as Steve Gerrard, David Thompson and my mate Jamie Carragher. We had all played for the youth team at various times and were all on the same wavelength. I am sure the foreigners had more trouble understanding the Scouse accent than we did their broken English!

Naturally with so much new talent in the squad it took us all a while to get to know each other – both as footballers and people. But over the course of the season we developed into a strong unit on and off the field. The addition of Emile Heskey, an £11 million signing from Leicester City towards the end of the campaign, gave us an even more formidable look as we pushed for a top three place and qualification for the European Champions League.

I got my first team chance with Liverpool towards the end of my first season as a professional. I was on the bench a couple of times before actually kicking my first ball in the Premiership – and my first inclusion among the seniors caught me totally by surprise.

The day before an away game at Sunderland, one of the coaches, Ronnie Moran, told me to bring my overnight gear next morning in case I was needed to travel with the first team. I left my stuff in the boot of the car and after training I was ready to drive home, assuming that I was not needed after all.

Ronnie saw me about to leave and said: 'Hasn't the gaffer said anything to you about coming with us?' I replied that he had not but he went to see the manager Roy Evans who confirmed I would be going up to the North East with the squad. I thought it would just be to gain some extra experience and never imagined I had a chance of being involved.

I was absolutely flabbergasted when I was named as one of the substitutes. Then I immediately thought of Mum and Dad and was concerned that they could miss my first big moment in the big time. I borrowed someone's mobile phone and called home. Mum insisted they could not possibly get there on time because there was only about an hour to go before the kick-off.

> ' *My performances and goals for Liverpool enabled me to fulfil my lifetime's ambition of playing for the full England side...* '

She explained that my Uncle John (dad's brother) and Auntie Julia – both mad keen Liverpool fans – were at the game and would give me the family support if I needed it. I looked up towards the 5,000 strong contingent of travelling fan and amazingly they were the first people I spotted.

I was not called upon during the Sunderland game but it was not too long before I tasted my first piece of action in the Premiership. It was an away game at Wimbledon which we had to win to stand any chance of staying with Manchester United in the race for the title.

We were 1-0 down and I was told to go and warm up in case I was needed. I sprinted towards the corner flag and before I reached it, Wimbledon scored a second goal. I was sent on immediately and managed to score my first senior goal. We ended up losing the game but it was a memorable occasion for me. Just to make it extra special I had become Liverpool's youngest ever goal-scorer, aged 17 years and 143 days. The following season I went from strength to strength and ended up as the Premiership's joint top scorer alongside Dion Dublin and Chris Sutton with 18 goals.

> **'I have received the occasional tongue-lashing from him [Phil Thompson]. Mostly he gets on to me about my defending ability.'**

My performances and goals for Liverpool enabled me to fulfil my lifetime's ambition of playing for the full England side and I know how much I owe to my colleagues, both on the playing and managerial side, for helping me to achieve the honour. Liverpool FC might not have enjoyed the same glory in recent times as in years gone by but I am pretty sure the trophy-winning days will return.

Already in my brief time at the club I have seen quite a few comings and goings and it was a sad day for me when Roy Evans left. He was the manager who gave me my first-team chance and I will always be grateful to him for that. He showed enormous confidence and faith in me when I was young and inexperienced.

I had not been in the first team too long when he called me over and said: 'While Robbie Fowler is not in the team, you'll be taking the penalties.' To put his trust in a 17 year-old boy was very flattering.

Roy left the club after a spell of sharing the managerial role with Gerard Houllier and on his departure the Frenchman took sole charge of the team. Things have become different under him. He is a very good communicator with the players and is meticulous in everything he does. Whereas with Roy Evans we would usually go straight into five-a-sides after our warm-ups, there is more emphasis on patterns of play and working on attacking and defensive drills with Gerard Houllier.

He also spends a lot of time watching opponents and if you were to ring Monsieur Houllier up on any night of the week, I would bet you would find him out at a game somewhere.

His handling of my injury at the start of the 1999-2000 was typical of the manager. He left nothing to chance after I suffered repeated problems with my hamstrings. He made sure I went to the best specialists in Europe and insisted I would remain patient and on the sidelines until he was absolutely certain I was free of injury worries.

The agonies I went through during that period at the end of the 1998-99 season and the start of the 1999-2000 campaign were more mental than physical. I was never in terrible pain. The hamstring strains were very niggling and for a while I lived with the uncertainty as to whether I would keep breaking down. Eventually I took a rest from the game in an effort to try and strengthen the muscles and rid myself of the problem once and for all.

" Liverpool FC might not have enjoyed the same glory in recent times as in years gone by, but I am pretty sure the trophy-winning days will return. "

> **' He [Gerard Houllier] is a very good communicator with the players and is meticulous in everything he does. '**

That made it frustrating for me because most of the time I was fit to play football but could not afford the risk of aggravating the complaint. I was itching to get back into action both to help Liverpool qualify for the European Champions' League and to secure my place in the England squad for Euro 2000.

But in the circumstances I had to abide by the manager's decision and trust in his judgment. He is a wise and experienced football man and from my dealings with him I feel sure the future of Liverpool Football Club is in safe hands.

While the boss gives us the benefit of his insight and meticulous planning, he has the ideal partner in Phil Thompson as his No 2. As a former Anfield favourite and member of so many successful Liverpool teams, Phil lives and breathes the club. He is very passionate about wanting us to emulate what he achieved as a player and is the voice you hear most on training and match days.

If he does not like something you have done or said, he will let you know in no uncertain terms. I have received the occasional tongue-lashing from him. Mostly he gets on to me about my defending ability. I know it is not the strongest part of my game and Phil is forever letting me know where I have gone wrong when it comes to closing down opponents and narrowing the options when they are in possession.

He gets a bit over-heated at times but when Phil speaks, you listen, not just because he shouts pretty loud but because he has a wealth of experience in this department from his playing days with Liverpool and England. As I keep repeating, I am still eager and willing to learn about the game and could not wish for two better tutors than Gerard Houllier and Phil Thompson.

One-to-One

Who is your favourite Liverpool player of all time?
John Barnes

When did you first play in a Liverpool team?
I played as an 11-year-old for their Under-12 team

What was your best Liverpool goal?
My hat-trick goal against Newcastle at the start of the 1998–99 season

What was your best match for Liverpool?
My hat-trick performance against Sheffield Wednesday in the 1997–98 season

How do you pass your time travelling to away matches?
Playing cards and chatting with my team-mates

Do you have your own spot in the dressing room at Anfield?
Yes, directly under the heater

Do you have any superstitions before a match?
I always put my right sock and boot on first

What do you wear travelling to matches?
For away games we have to wear the club suit – for home matches one of my own suits

How well do you sleep before and after matches?
I have no trouble getting to sleep before any game, but after a night match when the adrenalin is still flowing I sometimes struggle

What do you do after matches?
I normally go out for a meal with my family or friends

Did you ever stand on the old Kop end at Anfield?
No, I was usually playing football and didn't watch too many matches

Who is the biggest joker in the Liverpool dressing room?
Jamie Carragher

Michael Owen

' There had been speculation in the media that I had a chance of being named in the [England] squad, but to actually hear it confirmed was a moment I will never forget.'

ENGLAND

It was a chilly February morning as I stood on the fifth tee with my Dad at Chester Golf Club. It was strictly against club rules but I had left my mobile phone switched on for short time in case I got the call I was hoping for.

When it rang, the Liverpool coach Doug Livermore was on the line to tell me the amazing news. I was in the senior England squad for the friendly against Chile later in the month. I was only just 18 and had not even completed half a full season as a first-team player with Liverpool.

I am not normally an emotional person but this really stirred me. There had been speculation in the media that I had a chance of being named in the squad but to actually hear it confirmed was a moment I will never forget. My phone rang about another 20 times during the next 10 minutes from friends and colleagues offering their congratulations. Then, to the relief of the other golf club members, I switched it off.

Even my golf went to pieces. I had been a couple of holes up on my dad but he managed to pull them back Eventually I was able to compose myself to win the round and take a couple of pounds of prize money off him – as usual.

I had begun the season with just a couple of Liverpool appearances under my belt and my aim was to establish myself as a regular Premiership player while still continuing to learn my trade as a striker.

I had thought about playing for England but it was very much a long-term ambition that could be realised in two years' time at the earliest. Then I started scoring goals regularly for my club and began thinking to myself: 'Well, if this is what strikers like Alan Shearer do and it earns them a place in the England squad, then why not me?' It was the way players earned international recognition – establishing themselves as Premiership performers – and I was doing that for Liverpool.

When the England coach Glenn Hoddle told me I would be in the starting line-up after I reported for duty with the squad, I knew I was ready for it. I had always seized opportunities like this and was never once overawed. For as long as I can remember I had played in age groups with players a couple of years older than me and usually twice my size.

My attitude was just the same when I was picked to play for England. If I was good enough, I was old enough. I knew I could do well in senior international football. I looked around the Premiership and felt confident I was as good as anyone else. Nothing has ever overwhelmed me in football because I have always had real belief in my own ability.

'*I always aim as high as I possibly can and then even if I fall short of my targets, hopefully I will still achieve something.*'

I don't go around blowing my own trumpet in the media and never will, but I feel I can compete alongside and against the very best. I hope that doesn't sound too arrogant or conceited because that is not my style. It just reflects my total self-belief. I always aim as high as I possibly can and then even if I fall short of my targets, hopefully I will still achieve something.

When I stepped out at Wembley to face Chile, I became the youngest player in the 20th century to pull on a full England shirt. I was 18 years and 59 days and it was another marvellous milestone in my life. I had scored on my debut at all other England levels – for the Under-15s, 16s, 18s 20s and 21s – but I couldn't manage it this time and we were disappointingly beaten 2-0 by a very good Chile side.

I think I made a reasonable enough contribution, though, and the overall verdict on my performance was favourable. Straightaway my thoughts began to turn to winning a place in the squad for the World Cup finals later in the year. I was determined not to be ignored.

In the League game immediately after my debut I scored a hat-trick in Liverpool's 3-3 draw with Sheffield Wednesday. I felt it was one of my most important performances of the season. It was my way of showing that I was not complacent just because I had played for England.

' Nothing has ever overwhelmed me in football because I have always had real belief in my own ability. '

Things like that have never gone to my head. I am not at outwardly aggressive person but there is a determination inside me that keeps pushing me forward and makes me want to strive for new goals.

Joining up with England is a great experience. It makes you feel good inside that you are in among the nation's outstanding footballers. It also offers a nice change of routine from club football. It does leave you with a lot of spare time on your hands, though, because you are away from home for a week or more without your normal everyday activities to occupy you.

For home matches we are based at the Burnham Beeches Hotel and we are left with a lot of time to fill after training. There are snooker, pool and table tennis tables which help to keep us entertained and often we get a round or two of golf in so long as it is not too close to a game. I became very friendly with West Ham's Rio Ferdinand before and during the World Cup finals and he was my regular companion around the training camps. There is always a good team spirit among the squad with newcomers always welcomed into the fold. Alan Shearer and Paul Merson were particularly good at making me feel at home and passed on lots of handy tips.

After scoring my first international goal in a friendly against Morocco – it made me England's youngest-ever goal-scorer at 18 years and 164 days – my place in the World Cup squad was more or less assured though it still meant an anxious wait before the final 22 names were announced at our training base at La Manga in Spain.

The campaign in France did not get off to the best of starts for me. Despite a clamour in the media for me to be included in Glenn Hoddle's starting line-up, I had to settle for a place on the bench for the opening games but I was confident my chance would come.

It duly arrived when I was sent on against Romania and scored within 10 minutes of my arrival on the pitch and the newspapers were full of 'we told you so' messages to Glenn Hoddle. I was just happy to be involved and felt I had done enough to make the starting XI for future matches.

There was a lot of media attention on me at that stage and an amusing incident occurred when we had a golf day during a break in our World Cup training schedule. Paul Scholes and I challenged Alan Shearer and Teddy Sheringham to a four ball and the television cameras were allowed to film us for a couple of holes.

One-to-One

How do you psyche yourself up before a big international game?

I don't need to. Just pulling on the shirt and listening to the national anthem gets you in the right mood

What do you eat before a game?

Boiled chicken, rice and potatoes

Who is the loudest player in the England dressing room?

Gazza was always the funniest but Tony Adams makes the most noise when he is geeing everyone up before the kick-off

Who is your favourite England player of all time?

Gary Lineker

Who is your favourite world-wide international player of all time?

Pele

Which international goal gave you the most enjoyment?

The goal against Argentina in the 1998 World Cup finals gave me the most pleasure, but one I scored for England Schoolboys against Scotland was in my opinion a better individual goal

Which decade of football do you think was the best?

The nineties

Which is the best stadium you have ever played in?

Wembley

Who would be your ideal international strike partner?

Gary Lineker

Which was your best international performance?

The Argentina game in the 1998 World Cup finals

Which was the best all-time England team you have ever seen?

The one which got to the semi-finals of Italia 90

Michael Owen

> **' I am not at outwardly aggressive person but there is a determination inside me that keeps pushing me forward and makes me want to strive for new goals. '**

Word had already got around that I was supposed to be a bit of a crack golfer and all eyes were on me as we stood on the first tee. Needless to say, with the rest of the world looking on through the television cameras, I completely duffed my tee-shot and the ball skidded 30 or so yards up the course. Alan fell about laughing and jokingly muttered something like: 'See that. The boy wonder doesn't get everything right!'

I was still left with a pretty awkward lie for my second shot at the par three hole but I struck it to perfection and the ball landed about a yard from the pin. I turned to the television crews and said: 'I bet you don't show that on the programme tonight.' I was right. They didn't – just the shot of me messing up my tee-shot.

Back to the serious business of football, Glenn Hoddle decided to put me in his team from the word go after my goal against Romania and a 2-0 win over Colombia took us through into the second phase where we were to meet Argentina. No one needs reminding what happened next. We were beaten on a penalty shoot-out but I scored a goal in normal time that turned my life upside down.

It has been replayed hundreds of times on television and I have been asked to talk about it hundreds of times more but I never get tired of seeing it or describing it. So here we go one more time. I received a pass from David Beckham just inside the Argentina half with a defender breathing down my neck. My first touch needed to be good to steer the ball away from him, so I controlled it with the outside of my right foot and set off towards the opposition goal.

There was another defender between me and the goal and I felt if I could get past him, I might score. I knocked the ball behind him, which left me with just the goalkeeper to beat. Suddenly out of the corner of my eye I could see another player converging on the ball. Fortunately he was wearing the white shirt of England.

' I've come this far – no one is going to score now except me.'

It turned out to be Paul Scholes. For a second I imagined he was going to get there before me but I thought to myself: 'I've come this far – no one is going to score now except me.' As the keeper came off his line, I lifted it over his head into the net.

The England fans went wild and I was mobbed by my team-mates. However long I play football I will always be associated with that goal and why not? It will not be such a bad moment to be remembered for. The unfortunate thing was it did not take us through to the next round because Argentina beat us in the penalty shoot-out.

I was as gutted as any of the England players after the game about our exit from the competition but I was replaying my goal over and over again in my mind. On the coach going back to the airport for our flight back to our World Cup headquarters, I had a call from a friend on my mobile.

'You do realise what you have just done, don't you?' he said. 'That goal will change the rest of your life.' When I thought about it, I said : 'Yes. I suppose I have done something a little bit special.'

The reaction to it was way over the top. Suddenly I was being compared with Ronaldo as the greatest player on earth and described as the new Pele. I recalled all of that a few months later after a European Championship qualifier against Bulgaria at Wembley ended in a tame goalless draw.

The whole team got some stick for that performance and questions were being asked about whether I was worth a place in the team or if I was the ideal partner for Alan Shearer. From being out of this world there was suddenly a campaign to get me out of the side. But it taught me an important lesson. I realised how foolish it was to get too carried away by all the praise and glory and to become disheartened when the criticism is flying around. So far, I reckon I have managed to stay on a fairly even keel in my football career.

There was more criticism for both Alan Shearer and myself after the Euro 2000 qualifying game in Sweden which we lost 2-1 and the 1-0 defeat in a qualifying play-off game against Scotland at Wembley. Even though we beat the Scots on aggregate, there was an incredible uproar in the press with Alan and I getting most of the flak.

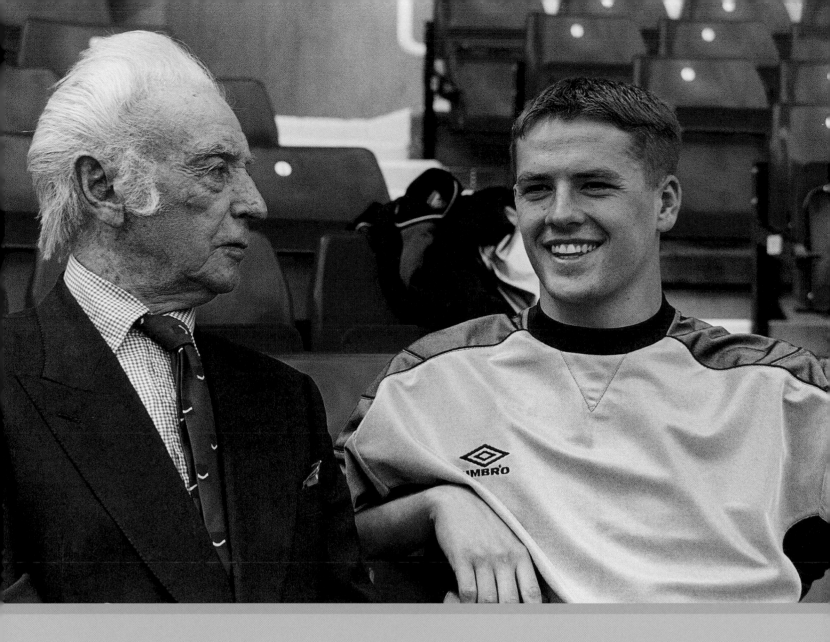

'I feel I can compete with the very best.'

It was even suggested I was not good enough because I could not kick the ball with my left foot – all because I failed to get a cross in from that side during the match. I couldn't believe what people were writing about me. – and these were the very same journalists who had been praising me to high heaven a few months earlier.

The difficulty in these situations for a striker is that you are not really in a position to influence a match if the service is not coming through from the rest of the side – unlike a midfielder who can grab a game by the scruff of the neck and alter the pattern of play. There are no shades of grey for a striker. You are either brilliant if you score spectacular match-winning goals, or worse than useless if you don't – even though not a single chance comes your way.

We all have to live with that – but I'll always back myself to finish up with my fair share of goals and praise before my career is over.

'*I realised how foolish it was to get too carried away by all the praise and glory and to become disheartened when the criticism is flying around.*'

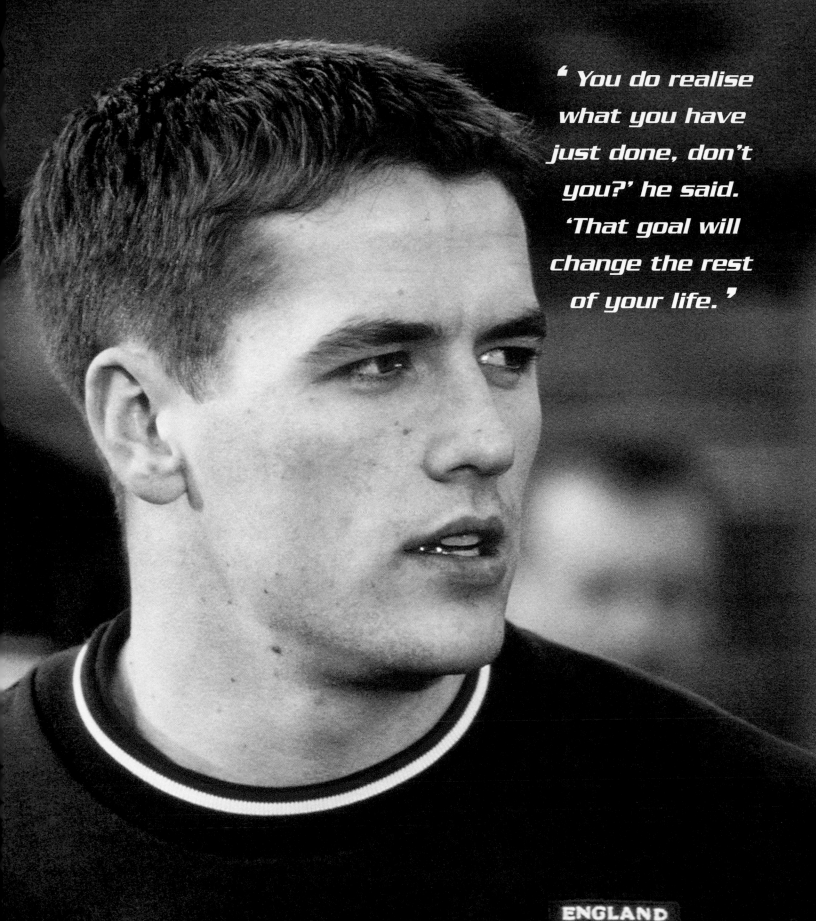

'You do realise what you have just done, don't you?' he said. 'That goal will change the rest of your life.'

41

' Gary Lineker was always my personal favourite whether he was wearing the blue of Everton or the white shirt of England. '

FANS

Most of my sporting life has been spent playing football, right through from my early days kicking a ball about in the park with dad and my brothers to turning out for the Liverpool and England senior sides. There is no better feeling than putting your boots on and going out and performing to the best of your ability.

Watching football does not satisfy me nearly as much – especially when I have been sidelined through injury – but I have always been a fan of the game for as long as I can remember. Dad's contacts at Everton meant the whole family always had plenty of opportunity to go to Goodison Park and I grew up supporting the blue half of Merseyside.

Gary Lineker was always my personal favourite whether he was wearing the blue of Everton or the white shirt of England. I always admired what seemed to be the effortless way he scored his goals and thought he handled himself superbly off the field as well. Andy Gray was another of my favourites – a completely different sort of striker but one who would set the pulse racing with the brave and fearless way he led the Everton attack at a time when they were bringing loads of honours back to Goodison.

I was always a massive England fan as a youngster and I remember being totally enthralled by the 1990 World Cup finals in Italy. I watched just about every game on television. England really captured the imagination of the whole nation that summer and were desperately unlucky to be beaten in a penalty shoot-out in the semi-finals by Germany.

Like all other England fans, Paul Gascoigne was my big hero during Italia'90. That was when he showed the world what a fantastic footballer he was and I doubt whether he has played better in his whole life. I still have his video in my collection and love to look back at the amazing things he could do during a game.

Unfortunately injuries and other problems have stopped him from extending his international career but I think we should still be grateful that we saw a player of his genius in an England shirt. I met him a few times when I first joined up with the international squad and while I did not get to know him all that well, I found him to be a smashing bloke.

When Liverpool played Glasgow Rangers in a testimonial game for the Scottish club's former manager Walter Smith, Gazza came into our dressing room before the kick-off and asked if he could swap shirts with me at the final whistle. For a player of his quality to want my shirt was a great honour and I got him to sign his Rangers jersey for me afterwards.

Swapping shirts after a game has never been a big thing for me. The Football Association give us two England tops per international – one to keep and one to exchange with an opponent – but I have always felt too embarrassed to go chasing after someone at the end of a game to ask whether I could have the shirt off his back.

Apart from football, I am a big fan of horse racing and boxing and even took part in the noble art when I was younger. Dad encouraged me to join Shotton Amateur Boxing Club because he felt it would help toughen me up, build my strength and be generally beneficial to me as a person because of the strict discipline required.

' Apart from football, I am a big fan of horse racing and boxing and even took part in the noble art when I was younger. '

The training was excellent and I actually stepped into the ring for a couple of fights. They went the full three-rounds distance and I won both of them on points – though not before collecting a bloody nose on each occasion. It was then I realised that the fight game was not for me, though I never really considered it as an alternative to football.

When I was moving out of the family home into my own place, I was clearing out some old stuff when I came across a plastic bag containing my boxing vest, headguard and gumshield. They were so tiny and reminded me how brave – and possibly foolish – I must have been to get into the ring to face lads who were much bigger than me.

I love watching big fight nights, either in person or on television, and my favourite boxer has always been Mike Tyson. I know he has done things outside the ring – and inside for that matter – which have damaged his reputation but when he was at his peak and devoted all his energies to beating his opponents, there was no-one to touch him.

I found it a bit strange to be on the receiving end of similar hero-worship at first – especially after returning from the World Cup finals in France when there was a huge crowd of fans at the airport all shouting my name. It was the same wherever I went for a few months after that, but I never really felt threatened by it.

The only real danger was that I would get a severe case of writer's cramp because of the number of autographs I was being asked to sign. I don't mind that. I go along with the saying that the time to worry is when people stop asking for your signature. It does amaze me, though, to see the same people outside the Liverpool training ground or at Anfield wanting you to sign for them day after day. Often they turn up for England training as well but I always try to oblige. I often wonder what they do with all of the scribbled bits of paper and signed pictures.

Even when I am out with my girlfriend Louise for a quiet meal it does not stop people from walking up to the table for an autograph. That can be a bit irritating but I always find it difficult to turn people away as long as they are polite and don't try to cause too much fuss.

The opposite was the case when we went out for a meal on one occasion with my Liverpool team-mate Jamie Redknapp and his wife Louise. A man and his partner sat on the next table to us and was perfectly well behaved – until it was time for him to leave. He shouted back to us: 'Everton are the greatest…Liverpool are rubbish!' which caused a stir through the whole restaurant. I thought it was really sad that someone should feel the need to behave like that in public and it was more embarrassing for him than it was for any of us.

" I was always a massive England fan as a youngster and I remember being totally enthralled by the 1990 World Cup finals in Italy. "

My mailbag is so big – though not as large as immediately after France 98 – that it would be impossible for me to read every single letter I get through the post. Most of them are just requests for signed pictures. I don't know how some of them find their way to me because a few of the foreign ones are addressed: 'To Michael Owen, Footballer, England.'

I get more than a few from girls asking me to marry them – all of which I have to politely decline. I get the really odd request sometimes like: 'Will you come to my birthday party next weekend? By the way, it is in Australia.'

Liverpool's fan base is so widespread that I get loads of mail from Scandinavia and the Far East. A lot want to know if they can join my fan club. I have to disappoint them because I don't have one. I don't really think they give a great deal of value for money, though at the time of writing this I am in negotiations with companies to produce my own internet website which will enable me to keep in touch with fans all over the world.

One-to-One

Which was the best game you ever watched as a fan?
England's victory over Scotland during Euro 96

Which of your favourite players did you meet as a kid?
Ian Rush and Ian Wright

Which was your most treasured autograph as a youngster?
Ian Rush

What was you most embarrassing moment with a fan?
After I signed an autograph for one young girl, she burst into tears and sobbed uncontrollably

How many autographs do you sign in a week?
On average about 300

Have you ever refused to sign anyone's autograph?
Not if I can help it, but sometimes I am in a rush to get somewhere and it might be difficult, or in a restaurant it can cause too much of a disturbance so occasionally I have had to say no

What was the best sporting event you have watched as a spectator (other than football)?
Mike Tyson's fight against Julius Francis in Manchester

What are the favourite charities for which you like to raise money?
Alder Hay Children's Hospital in Liverpool and the NSPCC

Who are the most appreciative fans you have played in front of, apart from Liverpool?
Newcastle United

Which were the worst fans you have played in front of?
At Barnsley when several fans invaded the pitch after they had a couple of players sent off

What is the funniest chant you have ever heard?
`He's Dutch, He's Red, He's off his ****ing head' (sung for my Liverpool team-mate, Erik Meijer)

What was the worst abuse you have had from a fan?
The local dustbin man gave me some terrible stick after England drew 0-0 in a Euro 2000 qualifying game in Poland

Michael Owen

> **" ...at the time of writing this I am in negotiations with companies to produce my own internet website which will enable me to keep in touch with fans all over the world. "**

Naturally my relationship with home-based Liverpool fans is great. I think they are always thrilled when a player comes through the ranks and establishes himself as a first-team regular, but it doesn't always work out like that. I have noticed there is a small contingent at Anfield who seem to be more appreciative of the big-money buys than the local-boys-made-good.

Let me give you an example. Robbie Fowler has been an incredible striker for Liverpool, scoring over 30 goals season after season. Yet when he was in partnership with Stan Collymore, it was always the £8 million signing who appeared to get more acclaim. There would always be groans whenever Robbie gave the ball away but the supporters were always ready to forgive Stan and couldn't wait to chant his name.

Maybe the fans' attitude is this: 'Well, the likes of Fowler and Owen, they are one of us. We are allowed to have a go at them without them being too offended.' I still find that a bit strange.

I am glad to say that the reception I get from away fans is quite good. I don't get booed on opposition grounds in the way that Alan Shearer does, for example. Not that it bothers Alan. Quite the opposite in fact, it spurs him on to try even harder. Immediately after the World Cup, I found I was getting applauded off the pitch at places like Southampton and Newcastle, which was nice.

As I remarked in an earlier chapter, I have had to put up with criticism, and I can live with that, but I went through a stage when it got a bit personal and was way out of order. Much of it was media-driven and I was suddenly being branded a 'cheat', supposedly because I had developed a habit of throwing myself to the floor to try and win penalties and even get opponents sent off.

It was pure nonsense. As a forward who relies on his pace and instincts to get past defenders, it is inevitable that I am going to win my fair share of free-kicks. It is one of the tricks of the trade nowadays to try to invite defenders into a challenge and lure them into bringing you down. But there is nothing dishonest or illegal about that and it does not amount to diving.

I felt deeply offended when I was being accused of cheating and I know my dad found it hard to accept as well. He and mum brought all the kids up the right way and taught us the importance of being decent and fair-minded in everything we do. I would never bend the rules on or off the football pitch. If I had to resort to that sort of behaviour, I would not bother playing the game I love.

" *I get the really odd request sometimes like:*
"Will you come to my birthday party next weekend?
By the way, it is in Australia." "

'*I found I was getting applauded off the pitch at places like Southampton and Newcastle...*'

' I realised I had suddenly been thrust into a celebrity spotlight far bigger than ever before. '

CELEBRITY

I knew my life was never going to be the same as soon as I returned from the World Cup finals in France in the summer of 1998. As I flew back with the rest of the England squad on Concorde the day after I scored that goal against Argentina, my feelings were mixed.

I was as disappointed as the rest of the squad that we had gone out of the competition in such an unlucky way but thrilled that I had scored one of the best goals of my career on the biggest possible football stage. The reaction had already been fantastic with some media pundits describing it as one of the finest World Cup goals ever seen.

My first inkling that I had suddenly become public property came when I called home soon after touching down on English soil again. My Mum answered the phone and joked: 'I wouldn't come home if I were you. There is an army of television crews, press photographers and reporters camped outside the front door waiting to talk to you.'

I called in at the Midland offices of my advisor Tony Stephens on the way back and he was able to confirm that the world had gone Michael Owen crazy. The phones had been ringing from 7.30 that morning from people wanting interviews and suggesting a variety of deals ranging from opening garden parties to major commercial sponsorships.

As I continued the journey back to my parents' house in Hawarden, I realised I had suddenly been thrust into a celebrity spotlight far bigger than anything I had experienced before. The previous season had been my first full one in the Premiership and I enjoyed the recognition that came with playing for one of the top clubs in the world.

' *I knew my life was never going to be the same as soon as I returned from the World Cup finals in France in the summer of 1998.* '

I was well-known in Liverpool and because of the popularity of the club overseas – particularly in the Scandinavian countries and the Far East – my fame had spread further afield. Now I was being portrayed as an international superstar and it felt strange.

But I made a conscious decision there and then that it was not going to go to my head. I was determined not to turn into some kind of pop idol. I was a professional footballer and that meant devoting my full attention to behaving in the disciplined way I had always done. That was vital if I was to continue to play the game at the highest level.

I got back home at around 2.30 in the morning and the gathering of people on the front lawn had grown even bigger. Even some of the neighbours had stayed up late to greet my return and they applauded me as I walked up to the front door. I was relieved to get inside and I talked with my parents about how my life was going to change and how we were going to cope with it.

A family holiday was discussed and we decided to go to Florida. We chose America because it is not a country totally obsessed with football and we felt we were more likely to be lost in the crowds. It more or less turned out that way. There were a handful of English holidaymakers who recognised me and wanted autographs but it was not a problem.

' ...there were tens of thousands of fans waiting for us at the airport, and the lobby of the hotel where we were staying was crammed with young supporters from morning until night. '

We were staggered when we rang home after several days to discover that one English newspaper had carried a picture of us relaxing by the pool – which proved that there really is no hiding place as far as the media is concerned. One paper went even further than that some time later. They tracked down a picture taken by an automatic camera of me coming down the log flume ride at Disneyland and splashed it across their pages. I don't know where they get their information from but you have to give them full marks for their detective work.

Once I reported for training with Liverpool, I thought it would be great to get back to normality. No such luck. The club had arranged their usual pre-season trip to Norway where we have a massive fan following. Things did get a bit frantic over there.

We always got a great reception on our arrival but this time there were tens of thousands of fans waiting for us at the airport and the lobby of the hotel where we were staying was crammed with young supporters from morning until night. The press called it 'Owen-mania' and said nothing had been seen like it since the days of The Beatles.

'I found it a little bit embarrassing
to have young girls screaming at
me and clamouring for
autographs...'

56

I found it a little bit embarrassing to have young girls screaming at me and clamouring for autographs and the rest of the lads took great delight in pulling my leg about it, but it was all taken in the right spirit. The last thing I wanted was to be treated any differently from the other players, but I think everyone accepted the hysteria as long as it did not affect our football preparations. It never did.

Back home the attention was just as great. Whereas I used to get a handful of mail each week from fans that my Mum dealt with, I was now getting two sackloads containing at least 1,000 letters. Fortunately, the club were good enough to provide the office staff to help handle them.

With the added fame came the fortune. Commercial companies of all shapes and sizes wanted me to endorse their products and I am not exaggerating when I say that several hundred offers came my way after the World Cup finals. I am fortunate enough to have an advisor who has the experience and know-how to sift through all the offers and sort out the ones that are the most suitable.

Eventually we decided on half a dozen very selective deals to promote me and various products in a way that would benefit us all. Now I was thrust into a world of television advertising and photoshoots which was new and exciting.

> ' *I was thrust into a world of television advertising and photoshoots which was new and exciting.* '

Walkers Crisps was one of the earliest deals I signed. To have my own brand, the 'Cheese and Owen' flavour, named after me was incredible. So was the chance to work alongside Gary Lineker who was always one of my footballing heroes when I was a kid.

The first thing I learned about television ads was how time-consuming they were. An advert lasting about 30 seconds can take anything up to two days to film. For the Walkers one, they had to cordon off a street in Liverpool city centre for part of the shoot and during a break in the filming one small kid manage to get onto the set to ask for an autograph.

I signed it for him and before I knew it hundreds more people were on the scene, clamouring for my signature. The proceedings came to a rapid halt while the area was cleared and I don't think I was very popular with the production team for causing the delay.

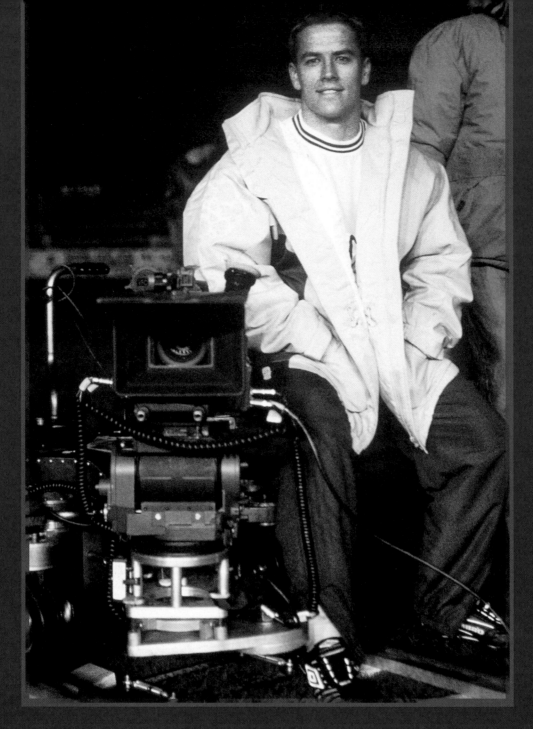

One of my most enjoyable projects was to take part in the production of my own soccer skills television series which went out on BBC and came second in the best children's programme awards for 1999. It was filmed over a couple of weekends at Stoke City's Britannia Stadium and gave me my first opportunity to teach young kids.

They were an outstanding bunch of boys and girls who had already developed their talent at the Brazilian Football Academy in Leeds under the guidance of coach Simon Clifford.

Because I was still recovering from a hamstring injury during the first few days of filming, I was not able to join in all the activities like shooting and tackling so I was able to devote more attention to chatting to the youngsters and developing a rapport with them. After they had got over their initial nervousness, we got on famously.

I hope they found the programme worthwhile and instructive – because I certainly did. They taught me one or two tricks with the ball that I am still trying to master. I wouldn't be at all surprised if I bump into one or two of them playing Premiership football at some stage in the future.

One-to-One

What is your favourite colour? Green

What are your favourite casual clothes? Tracksuit, trainers and tee-shirt

If you were invited onto a catwalk which designer clothes would you wear? Prada

What would be your ideal choice of car? A Jaguar XKR

How many photoshoots have you done in the last month? Four

If you could be anyone else, who would it be? Frankie Dettori

How often do you go shopping for clothes? Every three weeks or so

What is your best physical feature? My smile

And your worst? My hamstrings!

How often do you get your hair cut? Every three weeks

Which item of clothing would you definitely not wear? Y-fronts

A 'starring' role in a computer game manufactured by Eidos gave me an insight into the fascinating tricks of the trade of new technology. I never realised what went into the making of such games and again it was a slow and meticulous process.

I visited the production studios and was dressed up in a black lycra outfit to which was attached fluorescent markers. I then had to perform various football moves – including running, shooting, turning and celebrations – which were filmed before being converted into computer graphics.

I'll let you into a little secret here. Because of the time involved, an understudy had to be used for some of the shots. In my case this was Robbie Keane, who was a Wolves player at the time but who has since gone on to make a big name for himself after moving to Coventry for £6 million. I am sure Robbie did not mind filling my boots for a few hours. I did it myself when I was younger, standing in for Alan Shearer when he was making his computer game. I was a 16-year-old trainee at the time and the money came in very handy.

When my computer game was launched it gave me the chance to meet another world-famous computer star – the glamorous Lara Croft. She attended a press conference with me and I think there was an attempt at match-making when one journalist asked me what I thought of her. I replied: 'I hope to get to be as big as her one day.' This was not meant to be a reference to Lara's anatomy but a number of the journalists seem to found it amusing.

During an overnight stay at a London hotel before the Eidos announcement, I was on the receiving end of a very generous gift from the hotel management – or so I thought. A smart collection of Armani clothes was left for me and I assumed it was the hotel's way of showing their well-known guests their appreciation for staying there and encouraging them to do so again.

> ' One of my proudest moments was to be named BBC Sports Personality of the Year at the end of 1998. '

I mentioned to Tony Stephens that it was a smashing gesture even though the gear was a bit on the big side for me. But I would get it changed before I left for home. Just as I was about to go into the store to swap it, I got a phone call from my team-mate Jamie Redknapp saying his brother had left some Armani clothes at my hotel for me to collect and take up to Liverpool for him. He was just in time otherwise Jamie would have struggled to get into the Owen-sized outfit!

Being a famous footballer does have its perks, though. Every teenager dreams of owning a sporty Jaguar car and I was lucky enough to be offered one of their XKR turbo models as part of one of my sponsorship deals. It is a fabulous vehicle, but before getting behind the wheel Jaguar insisted I took an advanced driving test to make extra sure I could handle such a powerful machine.

A Day Out at Silverstone

I only discovered what driving a Jaguar was all about when I paid a visit to the Silverstone circuit just before the British Grand Prix and met up with the Formula One driving team of Eddie Irvine and Johnny Herbert during one of their test sessions.

It was an ear-shattering experience to walk through the pit lane while these monster cars were being revved up at full throttle and I discovered that ear-plugs are an absolute necessity for anyone working within the sport.

I got to sit in a Formula One car and I found it to be a bit of a tight squeeze. The seating area is so small and is specially moulded to the shape of the driver's body – in much the same way as my Umbro football boots are factory-made to my own particular size. Even someone as small as me found it difficult to fit my shoulders into the cockpit.

After photo and interview sessions with the motoring press, I was taken out for a spin around the Silverstone circuit by Johnny Herbert. Thankfully it was not in a Formula One car. Instead, I was Johnny's passenger in an XKR model identical to my own, though the journey was rather different to my leisurely trips to and from the Liverpool training ground.

Johnny put his foot down along the straights to reach speeds of up to 150 mph which I found quite exhilarating. It was when we approached the first corner that my heart leapt into my mouth. 'Oh my God!' I muttered to myself as he showed little sign of slowing down. He threw the car sideways into the bend at around 110 mph but seemed perfectly calm and in control.

It was quite a relief to come out of the corner still on four wheels and heading in the right direction. After negotiating that first curve I knew I was in safe hands and it made me realise what skills, nerve and courage were required by top class Formula One drivers. Three laps of the track were enough for me. I climbed out of the car and congratulated Johnny on his expertise. I was quite glad that I had chosen football as my career because life in that particular fast lane is definitely not one for me.

The route for my test was my normal journey from home to the Liverpool training ground. Most of the exam involves observation and spotting potential hazards – such as building sites where heavy plant machinery might be about to pull out in front of you, or even postboxes where someone might suddenly stop to drop in a letter. I managed to pass - but not with a perfect mark, which disappointed me a bit because with everything I attempt, I like to do it to perfection.

One of my proudest moments was to be named BBC Sports Personality of the Year at the end of 1998. It was a memorable day when I collected the award – for more reasons than one. Liverpool were playing away at Wimbledon that same afternoon and it was a game I would rather forget.

I missed a penalty in a 1-0 defeat and, to add injury to insult, I ended the game with a bruised and swollen eye which had been caused by a flying elbow from Wimbledon's Chris Perry. My eye had virtually closed by the end of the game but I was determined not to let either the disappointment of the final result or the pain and discomfort spoil the occasion.

'When my computer game was launched it gave me the chance to meet another world-famous computer star – the glamorous Lara Croft.'

I had to avoid the usual crowd of autograph hunters waiting outside Selhurst Park because if I had stopped for them I would never have made it to the programme. The BBC had sent a mini-bus and presenter Ray Stubbs to ferry me to the studios and I remember feeling a bit nervous as I entered the building because I had been tipped off beforehand that I was in with a good chance of winning the main award.

For the first time that year, part of the voting was going to be allocated to a telephone poll, which meant the final outcome was not known until the very last minute. When my name was called out as the winner, it was a terrific feeling. Fortunately, the swelling around my eye had gone down and I had to keep reminding myself to be careful not to drop the trophy and not to fluff my acceptance speech.

I managed to achieve both and when it was all over it was a privilege to see my name listed alongside all those illustrious sporting heroes of the past who had won the award before me.

It was an honour also to be asked by the Football Association to help promote England's bid to stage the World Cup finals in 2006 in the company of two football greats, Sir Bobby Charlton and Sir Geoff Hurst. We had to travel to Geneva to present our case to FIFA dignitaries and once more I found myself with the nerve-racking task of making a speech.

I did not find out until just before the presentation, otherwise I would have prepared something in advance, but I managed to scribble a few words down on a piece of A4 size paper and it seemed to be well received. I could not stop my mind wandering forward to 2006 and England playing in the World Cup final on home soil – what a pity that we lost out to the Germans yet again!

These off-field tasks have to be handled carefully if you are a high-profile footballer in the modern game. Not many of us have been prepared for public speaking or even the frightening task of having a microphone or tape recorder thrust under your nose to get your comments on any subject.

I have got used to it and learned the art of not getting caught up in too much controversy. I will still give my honest opinion on most things but have discovered that sometimes even the most innocent remark can be taken out of context and used in a distorted way.

All this goes with the territory of being a footballer – and I would not swap it for anything. It is true I have had to give up a few things in exchange for being a so-called celebrity – but it is a small price to pay. I cannot go to some of the public places I used to visit because of the fuss it could cause, but I still have my favourite haunts where I can go and enjoy myself in relative peace and quiet.

Basically I am a private person anyway. I much prefer a quiet night out with my family or close friends than attending a film premiere or nightclub opening. It was what I did before I became famous and I don't feel the need to be any different. At the same time, though, I cannot deny my 'new' world is exciting and the challenges it has given me have been unforgettable.

'It was an honour also to be asked by the Football Association to help promote England's bid to stage the World Cup finals in 2006 in the company of two football greats, Sir Bobby Charlton and Sir Geoff Hurst.'

'There were never many dull moments in the Owen household when I was growing up.'

> # *'We were taught to be keen and competitive in everything we did.'*

FAMILY

There were never many dull moments in the Owen household when I was growing up. With two brothers and two sisters for company, it meant I was always involved in plenty of family activities – most of them sporting ones.

We were a very close-knit unit and if either Terry, Andrew or I were playing football or Karen or Lesley were playing netball, there would always be a family fan club supporting them from the sidelines. Although my two brothers were a lot older than me, they always found time to join Dad and me in the park at the weekends. They could see how keen I was and recognised, even when I was tiny, that I had great potential as a footballer. They were determined to help me as much as they could.

We were taught to be keen and competitive in everything we did, but Mum and Dad always stressed there was a right way of doing things – both on the sports field and off it. They brought us up to be considerate and polite to others, especially to our elders, and I think those early habits we were taught have lasted us through to our adulthood.

Dad always encouraged us to have our own opinions, as long as we were not too argumentative, and tried to talk to us all on the same level. Now he reckons I insist on having the last word in any discussions we have, but I suppose that is the price he has had to pay for allowing me to develop a mind of my own!

As an ex-professional footballer, he was always there to offer me plenty of advice if I wanted it but never pushed me too hard and stressed that I should enjoy the game first and foremost. He did not fill my head with too much tactical and technical stuff but as a former striker himself, there was one lesson he continually drummed home to me.

> **" Mum and Dad always stressed there was a right way of doing things – both on the sports field and off it. "**

He emphasised the importance of following the ball in, whenever I or one of my team-mates had a shot at goal, and it is remarkable how many goals I was able to poach simply by being in the right place if ever the goalkeeper dropped the ball. My parents have always been there for me – even when I spent two years away at Lilleshall – and I shall never be able to repay them enough for that support.

Of my brothers and sisters, I spent more time with Lesley when I was younger because she was closest to me in age terms. When we were not pursuing our sporting interests, we would do all the daft things that kids enjoy around the house, like playing hide and seek and sliding down the stairs on cushions. I suppose I was very protective of her in those days because she was the baby of the family and I was her big brother.

We are all still very supportive of each other now, even though our careers have taken us in different directions. Terry, the oldest, works as an aero-fitter with British Aerospace in Chester, Andy is a fitness instructor in Liverpool, Karen is training to be a solicitor and Lesley is doing her A-levels in the sixth form.

When I started earning a lot of money from football, I decided the best way to invest my earnings was in property. We had always lived in the same family home but I knew the time would come when I had to branch out on my own eventually. I discovered that a plot of land was becoming available not far from where we lived and decided it would be great to have my own house built.

It took about 18 months to complete and I played an active part in its design. It was not a massive piece of land, which suited me because I did not want a vast garden to look after. One of my priorities was a snooker room, because that was a game I had come to enjoy since I was a kid.

After quite a few discussions with the architect, I agreed it would not be worthwhile sacrificing some lounge or dining room space on the ground floor, so he suggested we built the house on three storeys. That left me with enough room for my snooker room and a small gymnasium on the top floor. There are four bedrooms on the second floor – once of which contains a table tennis table and dart board. I like to have plenty of things to keep me occupied when my family and mates pop round for a visit.

> **" My brothers and sisters are all still very supportive of each other now, even though our careers have taken us in different directions. "**

Mum helped me with interior design and we have similar tastes as far as colours, carpets, wallpaper and furniture are concerned – though one particular idea of mine did not go down too well when I first suggested it. I woke up one morning and thought how fantastic it would be to be able to sit in my lounge at night with the main lights off and the room lit up with the dim lights of a fish tank.

At first I wanted it to occupy the full length of one wall but everyone thought that was a bit over the top. I settled for a half-sized one eventually and it blends in well with the rest of the décor. At first I filled it with very exotic fish but unfortunately several of those died and I have not replaced them.

Mum decided on the kitchen contents because it is not a part of the house I tend to use very much. I hate to admit this but I do not even know how to make a cup of tea or coffee. I don't drink them anyway – I prefer Pepsi Cola. I can boil a kettle for a pot noodle and have been known to warm up some food in the microwave but cookery is definitely not one of my specialities.

'*I hate to admit this but I do not even know how to make a cup of tea or coffee...cookery is definitely not one of my specialities.*'

> ' One of my priorities [in my new home] was a
> snooker room, because that was a game I had come
> to enjoy since I was a kid. '

I love my house and cannot see me ever wanting to sell it – even if my career should take me to another part of the country. I think I will always want to come back and live there.

At the same time as I moved into my first property, I decided to buy Mum and Dad a new house as well. It is barely half a mile away from where I live so they are always on hand to come and visit me. I was able to buy Andy the house next door to them while Terry stayed in the old family home, though he is thinking of moving because it is too big for him. I also bought Karen a flat in Chester, which meant the whole family was fixed up with new residence thanks to my success as a footballer.

I did not think twice about spending so much money on them because I knew whichever one of us had been in the same fortunate position, he or she would have done exactly the same. Dad set that example for us of sharing everything we had. If he won £30 on the pools or a few quid on the horses, he would insist on sharing it around the family rather than having a night out at the pub.

The only down side to having all these houses as far as Dad is concerned is that he has four lawns to mow which keeps him busy in his retirement! Oh, and there are eight cars between us for him to clean. He is never happier than when it is raining so he can sit and put his feet up.

I have always been very reluctant to talk too much about my girlfriend Louise publicly because, like me, she is a very private person and does not enjoy the public spotlight. I know I have to put up with it to some extent because it goes with my job, but I have never encouraged her to be featured in the newspapers – or my parents, for that matter – because they prefer to get on with their own lives without any intrusion.

I have known Louise since we were very young. My mum was friendly with her family for years because they only lived a few doors away from us. We both started infant school on the same day and I guess we developed a crush on each other early on. Over the years we started going out together on a very on-off basis but during my two years at Lilleshall, we did not even keep in touch with each other.

> *" Louise and I both started infant school on the same day and I guess we developed a crush on each other early on. "*

However, when I returned I had an inkling she was still keen on me because she had been asking my youngest sister Lesley about me when they met on the bus one day. Soon afterwards, I saw Louise one night in a local pub and asked if she fancied going out again and she agreed. Then I had to go on a pre-season trip with Liverpool to Ireland and I rang her a few times and we have been going steady ever since.

After the World Cup finals in France, there was a massive amount of media attention on me, which I had to expect, but inevitably they were interested in Louise as well, and wanted to know everything about us, such as when we were going to get married and would we be living together. I found it all a bit too much because I did not want to live out my romance in public.

All I can say on the matter is that we are happy with the relationship and both think we are too young to look too far into the future. We enjoy going out together – mostly with our respective families or friends for meals. Louise accepts that because I have grown up in a large family, I find it difficult for just her and I to go out together.

Louise only has one brother and she envies the fact that I have so many brothers and sisters and loves to be with us. We prefer to go out in a group, though we try to steer clear of nightclubs and bars because they can sometimes attract the wrong sort of publicity.

That is one thing I have learned about my social life. I always ask myself: 'If we go to this or that place, will the enjoyment we have be outweighed by the hassle I might get afterwards?' I always prefer to be cautious and stick to the places where I know I can be sure of a certain amount of privacy.

There is another special someone in my life who has become very much a part of the Owen family. He is my dog Bomber, a two-year-old Staffordshire Bull terrier, who has more or less taken over the household.

We have always had family pets. Over the years in our old house we had four hamsters, one rabbit called Carrot, a guinea pig called Clubber, and three budgerigars. I always wanted my own dog but Mum and Dad resisted giving in to me because they knew they would end up looking after it themselves.

While I was away at Lilleshall, I got friendly with a family who owned a Staffordshire Bull terrier and I fell in love with them as a breed. I knew when I returned home I would have to get one. 'Staffies' have a reputation of being fierce, aggressive and dangerous dogs, but I find that completely unwarranted.

I got Bomber when he was about six weeks old and he is the most friendly, lovable animal you could wish to meet. I spend hours with him walking in the woods near where I live, and in the summer he loves nothing better than when we take him to the Welsh beaches where he can romp in the sea.

One-to-One

How old were your parents when you were born? Mum was 28, Dad 30

What is your favourite home cooked meal? Steak and chips

Did you have school dinners or take sandwiches to school? School dinners

What was your favourite family game? Monopoly

Who walks the family dog? We all take it in turns

Do you help with the family chores around the home? No, but I know I should!

What was your favourite family outing? Alton Towers

What would be the ideal family holiday destination? Caribbean

Where did you go on you holidays when you were younger? Normally we just went on day trips but we had one great holiday in Ibiza

What did you miss most when you had to leave home at 14? My friends and family

Did you ever argue with your brothers and sisters? Nothing serious. It was usually over who was next to use the bathroom or which TV channel we should watch

What was the best piece of advice your dad ever gave you? It was a football tip about always following up a shot in case the goalkeeper dropped the ball

> ' **Golf was a game, which seemed to come very naturally to me from the word go, even though I never had any formal lessons when I first began playing.** '

HOBBIES

As soon as the school summer holidays began, there was only one place you would find me. For virtually the whole six weeks I would be at Hawarden Golf Club. Dad would drop me off at the course at eight o'clock every morning and I would stay there until six in the evening playing round after round of golf with my mates. Some days it would be 36 holes – on others we would even cram in 54. I was completely hooked on the game.

I would have £3 in my pocket at the start of the day – £2 for a steak and kidney pie lunch and £1 for a side-stake wager. Usually I would return home with £4, having scooped the prize money from my pals.

Golf was a game that seemed to come very naturally to me from the word go, even though I never had any formal lessons when I first began playing. I just developed my own swing from watching the professionals on television. My parents bought me my first set of clubs when I was nine – some Bernhard Langer Wilsons – and I certainly got my money's worth out of them because of the amount of time I spent playing during the summer months.

I must have played the best golf of my life at the age of about 13 when my handicap came down to nine. We were probably playing even better than that. My mates and I would usually go round in about three over par but there were a limited number of competitions for us to enter to get our handicaps down.

One of our group, Michael Jones, who was my best mate at school, has developed into a really good player and is thinking of turning professional. I guess I could probably have reached that standard myself if I had focused fully on the game but, of course, football was always my main priority and golf had to take a back seat once my career took off.

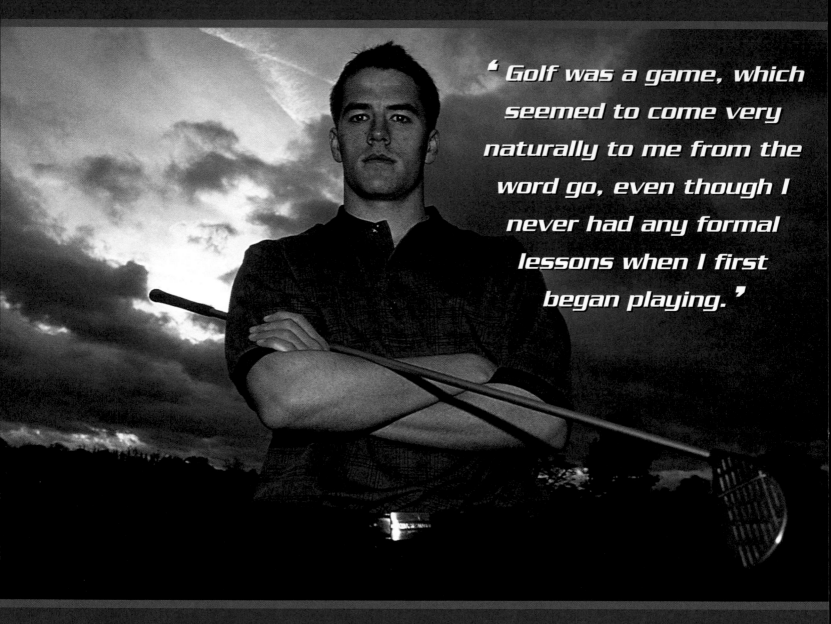

' Golf was a game, which seemed to come very naturally to me from the word go, even though I never had any formal lessons when I first began playing. '

I can still hit the ball off the tee a long way and that surprises a lot of people because of my size. Timing is more important than physical strength but it does surprise some people to learn that while I might not be the tallest at 5 ft 8 inches, I weigh over 11 stone, so I am by no means a weakling. It has annoyed Dad immensely over the years to keep reading newspaper reports, describing me as 'the tiny striker'.

When I was 13, I went for my first golf lessons with David Vaughan, a professional based at Llangollen, and he was amazed when I initially went to see him that I had achieved such a low handicap with the grip I was using. From my early days, I held the club like a baseball bat. He could not believe I had reached such a high standard but he immediately told me it would have to change if I wanted to improve even more.

He introduced me to the Vardon grip, which is one used by a large percentage of golfers, and for about a week it messed up my game completely. I thought each time I was about to hit the ball, I was going to let go of the club. After about a week I got the hang of it and have used it ever since.

Since becoming a professional footballer, golf has developed into more of a hobby than the total obsession it once was. I still try to play a couple of times a week, depending on my commitments with Liverpool and England, but have a strict rule that I do not play within two days of a match. It can be tiring on the legs to walk around 18 holes and I always spend the build-up to a game resting as much as possible.

My normal partner is my Dad and we have some very competitive matches with a pound or two as a side-stake. It is a very popular sport among footballers and comes in handy to wile away any spare time you have, when on tour with your club or country.

" I always believe that if you are playing any sport, even for fun, you play to win... losing can become a bad habit. "

My love for snooker stemmed from visits to the local snooker club in Hawarden with Dad from the age of eight. I thought I was pretty good at it then because I would beat him regularly. It was only a few years back when I was still beating him that he told me he would deliberately let me win when I was younger.

I have never felt like returning the favour and let him take a few frames off me. I always believe that if you are playing any sport, even for fun, you play to win. If you start to give anything away, losing can become a very bad habit.

I spend hours in my snooker room on the top storey of my new house playing against members of my family and friends. When the builders were near completion, I was worried at first that there would not be enough room for a full cueing action because the walls of the room went into the sloping roof of the building but they did an excellent job and still left me with enough space for an adjoining gymnasium.

My passion for horse racing was another I inherited from Dad. Horses are beautiful animals and I often used to go to the local riding school as a kid. Little did I realise then that one day I would be the proud owner of a couple of racehorses myself.

The idea to buy them first came to me when I attended the Professional Footballers' Association dinner in April 1998 to receive the PFA Young Player of the Year award. I was sitting at the same table as the former England football captain David Platt, a keen racing fan, and horseowner.

I spent the whole evening talking about the sport and he said he would introduce me to John Gosden, one of the country's top trainers based at Newmarket. I never had any intention of becoming an owner but I began to like the idea. At first some people tried to put me off, saying I was too young and it did not really present the right image for me to become involved in racing.

But I remained adamant. At first I was just going to get the one and John Gosden said I should stick to getting a filly because even if they had no real racing ability, you could always breed from them. I got a call from John one day while I was on England duty at Burnham Beeches, saying he could get either a colt or a filly for me at a very good price.

" *Little did I realise then that one day I would be the proud owner of a couple of racehorses myself.* "

I pondered over the choice for a while and then decided: 'It's no good. I've got to have them both.' So I agreed to the deal there and then. When I eventually saw them, they were really tiny – no bigger than ponies and with no muscle definition. Most Sundays now when I have some free time, Dad and I visit the stables to see them. We have watched them grow from babies into beautiful racing specimens and we have developed a real affection for them.

When it came to giving them their racing names, the filly did not present too much of a problem. I called her Etienne Lady – after the French town where I scored the goal against Argentina in France 98. The colt's name took a bit more working out.

I have mentioned before that the Owens like to do as much as possible as a family. So I decided to try and include them all in my choice for my second horse's name. I came up with Talk to Mojo. Each letter represents the initials of my brothers, sisters, Mum and Dad – Terry, Andrew, Lesley, Karen; Terry Owen; Michael Owen and Janette Owen. It sounds a bit obscure but it has made them all feel as if they own part of the horse.

'My love for snooker stemmed from visits to the local snooker club in Hawarden with Dad from the age of eight.'

> *" I tend to get bored very easily and love to have people around me. "*

My interest in racing also gets a mention in my house name. I called it Ten Furlongs – the figure being my shirt number and furlongs being the measurement used for some race distances. I do like a bit of a flutter on the horses and study form but it only amounts to a few pounds a week. I could easily watch horse racing and not have a bet.

I spend a lot of my spare time at home and get a constant stream of visitors from my family, Louise and other friends. That is important to me because I tend to get bored very easily and love to have people around me. My attention span is also very short and I cannot sit for hours on end watching television. I have to get up after a while and have a game of darts or snooker.

One-to-One

What is your best snooker break?	64
What is your best round of golf?	72 (at Curzon Park, Chester in 1999)
When did you play your first round of golf?	Age 9 at Hawarden Golf Club
What is the best film you have ever seen?	Cool Running
What was the first record you ever bought?	`Nessun Dorma' by Luciano Pavarotti (during Italia '90)
What is the best book you have ever read?	The BFG by Roald Dahl (it was read to us by a schoolteacher)
Which film star would you like to meet?	Eddie Murphy
Which is your favourite TV programme?	A Question of Sport
What is your favourite type of restaurant?	Chinese
What would you take with you on a desert island?	My golf clubs
Who would your ideal golf partner be?	Colin Montgomerie
What is the best restaurant meal you have ever eaten?	Grilled salmon and broccoli

Michael Owen

But there was one track which I did rush out and buy as soon as I heard it. When I scored a goal for England Schoolboys against Brazil at Wembley, they replayed the highlights at the end of the Sky TV coverage to the accompaniment of a song called 'Pure' by the Lightning Seeds. That remains one of my all-time favourites – as does 'Nessun Dorma' by Luciano Pavarotti because it reminds me so much of the World Cup finals in Italy in 1990. Who would have ever thought I was a fan of opera!

As you have probably guessed, my interests outside of sport are fairly limited. I have always preferred to do something lively, even if it is just pitting my wits against the rest of the family in a game of Monopoly or Scrabble. Apart from the time I spend with Liverpool, I am never happier than when I am at my own home.

As well as being somewhere to live, it is my playhouse where I can indulge in most of my favourite pastimes. If only it had a bigger garden, I could have built my own golf course. Perhaps not. It would not have been fair on Dad to expect him to cut the grass…

> **'I reached the stage where I began to wonder: "Am I ever going to get an injury?" It was a foolish thing to even contemplate.'**

FITNESS

One of the first things I was taught as a professional footballer is that you can never expect your life to be one smooth, uninterrupted success story. Even for someone like me who has made such massive progress so early in my life, the game has to contain some setbacks.

Injuries area an occupational hazard for any player and I doubt whether there has been a single professional who has gone through a career without suffering a prolonged spell on the sidelines and undergoing treatment. However, I reached the stage where I began to wonder: 'Am I ever going to get an injury?' It was a foolish thing to even contemplate.

Towards the end of the 1998-99 season I began to suffer a few twinges in my right hamstring – nothing too severe at first – but it went with a vengeance in a Premiership game at Leeds in April 1999. I was told straightaway by some of my more experienced colleagues that a torn hamstring was an injury that could not be rushed and it would need time and patience before it was fully healed.

I was quite prepared to take on board that advice but could not have foreseen the difficulties that lay ahead. I worked really hard for most of that summer, having treatment and doing exercises to try to make sure I would be fit for the new season. It was to no avail because I kept having niggling problems with my right leg.

Eventually Liverpool decided that a different course of action was needed. It was felt a visit to the Munich clinic of Dr Hans-Muller Wohlfahrt would benefit me and cure the hamstring once and for all. His name had come up during conversations with my then German club-mate Karlheinz Riedle, who pointed out the success rate the doctor had achieved working with other sports stars such as Linford Christie, Boris Becker, Steffi Graf and Jurgen Klinsmann.

I also discovered that Dr Wohlfahrt had been responsible for saving the career of the Spanish golfer Jose Maria Olazabal, who literally had to learn to walk again after a crippling injury. Being a massive golf fan, I knew that if he was responsible for that kind of recovery, I was in safe hands.

There was a lot of hysteria in the media around the time of my visit to Munich about the sort of methods which were used by Dr Wohlfahrt. They claimed I was going to be injected with sheep's blood, calves' livers and various other weird concoctions. Apparently, he did use some alternative methods in his treatments but not with me. The newspaper reports were absolute nonsense and I could not help having a good laugh about them.

' *The doctor felt my problem was my posture and basically I had not been careful enough with the way I had carried myself or even sat down for the first 19 years of my life.* '

I told the German doctor that I was still feeling some discomfort in my hamstring and there was a fear that it had torn again. He was able to allay my worries on that straightaway by telling me it had merely gone into spasm. Dr Wohlfahrt then explained in detail how he believed in treating the source of an injury rather than the actual complaint itself.

He felt my problem was my posture and basically I had not been careful enough with the way I had carried myself or even sat down for the first 19 years of my life. It had caused my pelvis to go slightly out of line and that was putting unnecessary pressure on my hamstrings.

He pointed out the need for proper relaxation in between training sessions and the need for hot baths, the correct way to sit in a chair and even the right position for the seat in my car. He gave me a series of stretching and strengthening exercises and told me it was important to continue them for the rest of my career.

I came away feeling re-assured that the injury was not a cause for long-term concern. It was incredible that the press were already starting to refer to me as 'injury-prone' when in fact it was the only problem I had experienced since the time I started playing football as a small boy. I was more determined than ever to put the matter behind me. That meant sticking rigidly to my exercise programme to ensure that both my hamstrings were strong enough to carry me through my career.

I had to make one more visit to see a Harley Street specialist before I could feel satisfied that the hamstring strains were not going to be an on-going worry. It involved a rather unusual test which came as a bit of a shock in more ways than one. The specialist stuck pins in my foot and along the length of my leg and sent an electric charge through the nerve.

It was a way of establishing whether there was any abnormal defect. He could find nothing and it was a big relief to have confirmed what was suspected all along. All the hamstring problems I had suffered since the original tear had been minor ones in different parts of my leg. Further tests showed there were weaknesses in some muscles and imbalances in others and emphasised the need to carry on my exercise regime to continually build up the strength in them.

'It was incredible that the press were already starting to refer to me as "injury-prone" when in fact it was the only problem I had experienced since the time I started playing football as a small boy.'

'There had been a lot of misleading newspaper reports that I was suffering from 'burn-out' as a result of playing too much football so soon in my career.'

There had been a lot of misleading newspaper reports that I was suffering from 'burn-out' as a result of playing too much football so soon in my career. While it is true I had played over 100 games for my club and country and was still only 19, I did not feel I was overstretching myself. When you are young and eager to make an impression, you want to play as much football as possible.

However, the body does have a way of sending out warning signals and I reckon the hamstring problem was its way of telling me I had to take action before it became a more serious one. I have always been aware of the need to look after myself. I have plenty of rest, I sleep well, eat the right things and rarely touch any alcohol.

' A footballer's life is not all about big wages and glamorous lifestyles. We have to put in our fair share of graft on the training ground... '

I am even more aware of taking care of my body since my injury because hopefully there is a long and successful career ahead of me. A footballer's life is not all about big wages and glamorous lifestyles. We have to put in our fair share of graft on the training ground, especially during pre-season, and if you try to skip the workload, you soon get found out when the real action starts on match days.

At Liverpool, there is an emphasis on trying to make training as enjoyable as possible, while at the same time gaining maximum benefit from it. Gone are the days when footballers used to have to slog their way around lap after lap of a football field. Most of the work now is carried out with a ball and designed to emulate match-type situations.

Once the season is underway, it is just a case of keeping your fitness level up to a peak. When you are playing two matches a week, there is not too much need to push the body too hard, but if there is no midweek match, we can usually expect a bit of a gruelling session on a Tuesday with some sprinting and longer running.

I hope I don't paint a picture of hard-pressed, overworked individuals who are driven like slaves around a training ground. Of course there are pressures, both mental and physical, which can leave you drained at times but I don't think there is a single footballer who would change his life for any other. What could be better than being paid handsomely for taking part in the greatest game in the world?

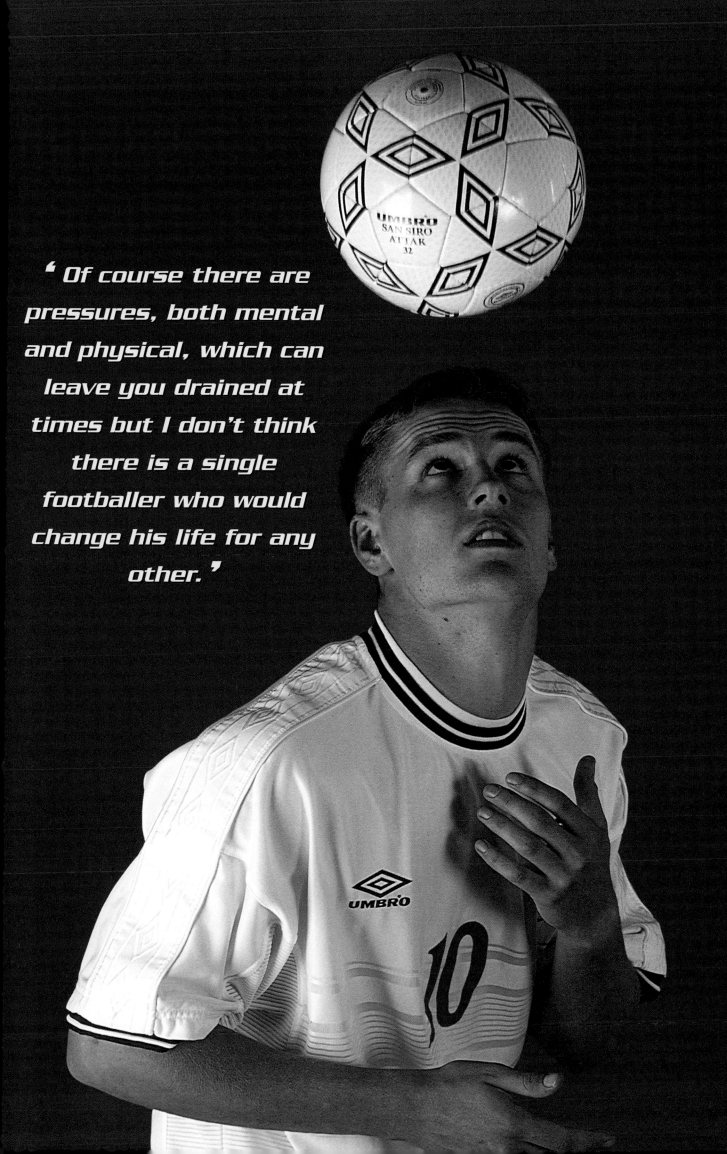

' Of course there are pressures, both mental and physical, which can leave you drained at times but I don't think there is a single footballer who would change his life for any other. '

PROFESSIONAL

Footballers are very much creatures of habit. We all have our set routines and tend to stick to them quite rigidly. That is particularly true on match days when our lives tend to fall into a strict pattern.

Players' preparations are carefully worked out in the modern game and in the build-up to a big match everything tends to run to a clockwork precision, so that when the kick-off arrives we are prepared physically and mentally for what lies ahead. I have my own routine that varies only according to the time the game starts.

This was my timetable of events on the day we played a vital local derby game against Everton at Goodison Park in an evening kick-off near the end of the 1999-2000 season. They are always very passionate occasions and this was no exception. It was especially important for us because we needed to win to maintain our push for a qualifying place in the European Champions League.

Friday 21 April 2000

9.00 am Woke after a sound night's sleep. I very rarely eat breakfast because it often makes me feel sick if I am in a hurry to leave the house. I had a bowl of cereal he night before to make sure I don't start the day feeling hungry. After a shower I change into my Liverpool club suit which is what all the players must wear for away games.

10.15 am We have to report to Anfield for 11.15 so I give myself ample time for the 45-minute drive. I call into a shop near my home for a bottle of mineral water on my way to the ground.

11.15 am We leave Anfield on the team coach for a local hotel. Even though this particular away match is right on our doorstep, the club management want us to spend the hours leading up to the kick-off together so we can relax and remain free from any distractions.

12 noon We arrive at the hotel and are taken on a half hour walk through the grounds to stretch our legs.

12.30 pm We all sit down for lunch. I stick to my usual choice of boiled chicken, potatoes, rice and a covering of bolognese sauce. The timing of the meal is important because we have to make sure it is fully digested before the game kicks off.

1 pm We go up to our hotel rooms to rest. I never sleep on the afternoon before a night game because I always wake up feeling drowsy and not quite with it. It also tends to disrupt my sleeping pattern later on in the evening. My room-mate Jamie Carragher usually nods off for a couple of hours but on this occasion we both settle down to watch the First Division game between Charlton and Portsmouth on television.

4.30 pm We get a call from the coaching staff and report back to the dining room for a light snack. Cereals, toast, rice pudding and fruit are on the menu. I have some toast and a banana and while most players have a pot of tea, I never touch the stuff and stick to mineral water. We return to our rooms to get changed into our suits for the game.

5.45 pm Gerard Houllier gathers the players together for our team meeting. The side has been selected the day before and we have worked on tactics and set-pieces so the manager has no need to go into too much technical detail. He stresses the importance of the game, not just because it is a local derby and means so much to the fans but because of the need to consolidate our position in the top three. He underlines how important it is not to get too carried away by the high passions of the derby game. Three players were sent off in the match against Everton earlier in the season and he did not want a repeat of that. 'If you lose your heads, there is no chance of us winning this game,' he insisted.

6.15 pm We leave the hotel for Goodison Park. Each of the players has their own particular seat on the coach. Mine is towards the back, near the kitchen area and faces away from the driver. I have sat in it ever since I broke into the first-team squad. It is not so much a superstition – just a habit that never seems to change. There is not much talk among the players on the journey. We are all focusing hard on the game now. Plenty of liquids, such as water and lucozade, are being drunk.

6.40 pm We arrive at the ground and get the expected hostile reception from Everton fans. Last season it was particularly bad and we were spat at as we made our way from the coach to the players' entrance. Now there are two metal barriers leading from the steps of the bus to the doorway to offer us more protection. I sort out tickets for my family and friends. We are allowed to have two complimentaries and can buy six others. I have no trouble allocating them for a match like this.

6.45 pm Most of the players go out and have a look at the pitch but it is something I have stopped doing since I had the problems with my hamstrings. I find it much more valuable to have a massage from one of our two masseurs, Gary Armer, who spends about 10 minutes working on both of my legs. Then I jump straight onto physio Dave Galley's bed and he puts me through a rigorous routine of stretching exercises.

7.10 pm I start to get into my match gear, sticking carefully to my superstition of always putting my right sock, shin pad and boot on before the rest of my kit. We all leave the dressing room for a warm-up session with one of the coaching staff, Sammy Lee. I tend to go out in tracksuit bottoms because it enables me to warm up my leg muscles a lot quicker.

7.15 pm The warm up starts with a slow jog and develops into a sequence of jumping and stretching movements, then some three-quarter pace running and finally some flat out sprinting. Then we spend around 10-15 minutes getting a feel of the ball before returning to the changing rooms.

7.45 pm There is 15 minutes to go before the kick-off and the tension starts to mount. The manager goes around to each player to deliver some few final instructions. He tells Emile Heskey and I to work closely together, keep looking for each other and whenever possible to run at the Everton defence with the ball. Ours is normally a quiet dressing room but before this derby game there is more noise than usual. It means such a lot to Scousers like Jamie Carragher, who have grown up knowing exactly what the match means to the fans. He is shouting to the other players and getting them geed up. I always get a few butterflies just before I go out but once on the pitch I feel reasonably relaxed and focused.

8 pm–9.50 pm It is a typically hard-fought derby game, very competitive with neither side willing to concede anything. I manage to get three half-decent chances but fail to convert them. Each time I force the goalkeeper Paul Gerrard to make a save but am disappointed not to get the all-important goal. The match finishes goalless but ends with a moment of controversy. With a few seconds remaining as our goalkeeper Sander Westerveld tries to clear the ball, it hits Don Hutchison on the back and loops into the net. To be honest, I do not see the incident because I am looking the other way. The referee Graham Poll disallows the 'goal' because he claims he had already blown the whistle for full time as our keeper kicked the ball. There are protests from the Everton players and fans but the referee stands by his decision.

10 pm The mood is a bit subdued back in the dressing room because we were confident of claiming all three points. A draw against our old rivals on their own pitch would normally be quite satisfying but the manager is disappointed because the extra points would have been invaluable in our Champions League bid. He may be a quiet and thoughtful individual to the outside world, but Mr. Houllier is a real winner and is desperate to see Liverpool prosper. He tells us we have three days off which is a pleasant surprise. Normally I would go into the training ground the day after a game for a massage but because of the time off, I decide to have one immediately after the game. It is to avoid any stiffness and soreness in my muscles. I am extremely careful of my hamstrings because I do not want any further problems now that the injury has been resolved. I have a shower and board the coach back to Anfied.

11.05 pm I drive home, still replaying some of the incidents from the game over in my mind. Once back in the house, I switch on the television and watch some of the highlights on Sky Sport.

12.00 midnight. I am tucked up in bed and it does not take me too long to fall off to sleep.

'To play with and against the very best players in the game in front of big crowds every week is the sort of experience money cannot buy.'

Dream Team

I was fortunate to have been able to launch my career as a first-team player at Liverpool at a time when the Premier League had reached new levels of excellence and excitement and established itself as one of the greatest domestic competitions in world football. To play with and against the very best players in the game in front of big crowds every week is the sort of experience money cannot buy.

Obviously money comes into the whole equation because without the millions of pounds pumped into the sport by the television companies and other major sponsors, we would not have been able to attract to this country the quality performers who, in years gone by, would have headed for Italy, Spain or Germany.

But having set the ball rolling and imported the big overseas players, top clubs like Liverpool, Chelsea, Arsenal and Manchester United have created a workplace where the world stars want to be. They know that our football is flourishing, the skill levels are high and the rewards are enormous.

I feel privileged to be part of this environment and with a fair amount of good fortune and a lot of hard work, I know I can continue to make my mark at the top level for many years to come. It has been a fascinating and productive introduction to the professional ranks. Each week playing for Liverpool, I come up against opponents who present new and exciting challenges. To be able to pit my wits against them and survive at this level means I can only improve as a footballer.

So I thought it would be fun to name my current all-star line-up from the Premiership. Picking dream teams has become a favourite pastime for football fans and prompts hours of discussion and argument. To avoid accusations of favouritism or the risk of upsetting any team-mates I might be forced to leave out, I have decided not to include any Liverpool players in my side. In a 4-4-2 line-up these are my selections:

David James (Aston Villa)

' David is a supremely confident individual with tremendous belief in his own ability. '

I know from my time with him at Anfield what an outstanding goalkeeper he is. He was superb for most of his spell at the club – a real commanding character who could come and catch crosses as far out as the edge of the penalty area and produce some amazing saves on his line.

Unfortunately and undeservedly, he will probably be remembered by most for the dodgy period he had when every little error he made was highlighted and all the good things he did were overlooked. David is a supremely confident individual with tremendous belief in his own ability but I think the criticism started to get to him during the final stages of his Liverpool career.

It did him a power of good to have a change of club and Villa gave him the chance to relaunch his career. In his first season at Villa Park, he confirmed his reputation among the top keepers in the country and the calls for him to be given an England recall were not misplaced.

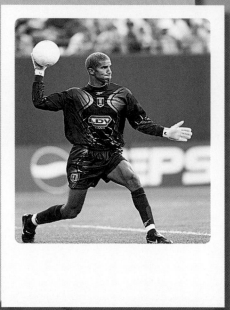

Gary Kelly (Leeds United)

' He is very quick, especially when it comes to chasing back and getting in a recovering tackle. '

Like all good full-backs, Gary knows his priority is to defend and prevent his opponent from making too many inroads into the back four. He is very quick, especially when it comes to chasing back and getting in a recovering tackle.

But there is another side to his game as well. Modern full-backs, even in a 4-4-2 system, have to be able to venture forward and offer support whenever their side is on the attack and Gary can do this to great effect. He crosses a good ball and is not afraid to have a crack at goal either.

It is easy to overlook the fact that Gary is still only in his mid-twenties but he has crammed a load of experience into his career so far, both with Leeds and the Republic of Ireland international side.

' Not many strikers can out-sprint him in a race for the ball. '

He is one of the most difficult and awkward central defenders I have come up against in the Premiership He seems to have this clever and uncanny knack of being able to nudge you off balance at a crucial time and most of the time gets away without having a free-kick awarded against him.

That's all down to his experience. He became a permanent fixture in the famous Arsenal back four which proved so difficult to break down and was the cornerstone of their years of success in the Premiership but has also proved himself at international level with England.

He is one of the quickest defenders around. Not many strikers can out-sprint him in a race for the ball. He is strong in the tackle and in the air and because of his pace tends to be able to nick the ball away from strikers with the quickness of his feet rather than just with brute strength.

' Tony is a real leader of men. Even when he is not captain, he stirs everyone up... '

He seems to have been around forever and, although he has been troubled with injuries in recent times, Tony shows no signs of being over the hill. I can think of no better barrier in the centre of my Dream Team defence than the Gunners' partnership of Adams and Keown.

He is a strong man – both mentally and physically. Sitting in the England dressing room before a big international game, it is comforting to know the Arsenal captain is going to be out there with you, putting his neck on the line if the going gets tough. Tony is a real leader of men. Even when he is not captain, he stirs everyone up and gets you in the right mood in the final few minutes before kick-off.

He takes those leadership qualities out onto the field with him and is never afraid to go in where it hurts. He may not be as quick as he once was but his positional play is so good, you very rarely see opponents get the wrong side of him.

Denis Irwin
(Manchester United)

' He never seems to get flustered... '

Like his international partner Gary Kelly, Denis is primarily a very good defender who knows that his first objective is to tame his winger and stem the source of opposition attacks. He does this and still manages to get up to support his forwards.

He never seems to get flustered and I have seen him step forward to convert some valuable penalties for Manchester United at crucial times in very important matches. That shows what a cool customer he is.

In over 10 years at Old Trafford, he has won loads of medals and trophies and I'll be more than satisfied if I can emulate what he has achieved when I reach the same stage of my career.

David Beckham
(Manchester United)

' He does not have to beat his defender. He just needs half a yard of space and whips over his centres. '

Everyone knows what an exciting player David is. What they don't always realise is how hard he works during a game. I have watched him closely in many matches for United and England and he never stops chasing back and closing opponents down.

But that is typical of the United team. You know when you play against them that you are not going to get a spare second on the ball without someone snapping at your heels. It says a lot for David's fitness that his overall work-rate does not stop him from producing real quality in and around the opposition area where he can cause most damage.

His crossing ability is out of this world. It must be great for a striker playing with him every week to know that he will deliver the ball where you want it and when you want it. He does not have to beat his defender. He just needs half a yard of space and whips over his centres. It is almost impossible to stop him, even when you know exactly what he is about to do. His free kicks and corners are the best in the Premiership.

> **'You cannot get near him when he is on the ball and for such a huge man he has incredible skill.'**

I found it really difficult to chose between Vieira and Manchester United skipper Roy Keane for one of my midfield positions. There is so little to choose between them but I went for the Arsenal man in the end because of his greater power.

The thing I noticed about the Frenchman when I first came up against him was how massive he is. The record books say he is 6ft 3in tall but he appears to be much bigger than that. You cannot get near him when he is on the ball and for such a huge man he has incredible skill.

He can win the ball and use it effectively and his height is invaluable to Arsenal in both penalty areas. I think he was a little bit unlucky to get caught in the refereeing clampdown when he first arrived in this country and it landed him in a lot of disciplinary trouble but I think he has learned to control some of the worst sides of his temperament.

> **'When he is on song, he is unstoppable. He is world class.'**

Of all the current players in the Premiership outside Anfield, he is probably my favourite. He has just about everything you need in a midfield player – energy, skill, aggression and the ability to score goals from anywhere.

I have worked with him at close quarters in training with England and his ability is quite frightening. You should see how hard he hits the ball when he shoots at goal. There is not only power. It dips and swerves and wobbles in the air. I would not like to be a goalkeeper on the receiving end of one of his efforts.

But he does not just score goals from a distance. He has the gift of being able to time his runs into the penalty box to sniff out chances from close range as well. When he is on song, he is unstoppable. He is world class.

> **"He catches the eye because he has a commodity you don't find too often these days – the ability to dribble past defenders."**

He has come of age in the last couple of seasons among a team of very exciting Leeds youngsters. He catches the eye because he has a commodity you don't find too often these days – the ability to dribble past defenders.

Some people think he will make a better central striker at some stage in his career but I reckon the Australian youngster is most dangerous when he picks up the ball from deeper positions and runs at defenders. He just seems to be able to drift past them effortlessly without any obvious change of pace.

He finishes well with a good shot in both feet and gets his fair share of headed goals. He is not powerfully built but stands up to the physical side of the game and is not afraid to get his foot in – even though he would admit tackling is not the best part of his game.

> **"You do not really appreciate how good Alan is until you have played alongside him."**

There is not too much you can say about Alan that has not been said a million times before. He is the complete striker. He packs an incredible wallop in his shots, particularly with his right foot, is strong in the air and knows how to lead the line and bring others into play. He is also the best penalty-taker I have ever seen.

I have learned an awful lot from just watching Alan – both on and off the field. I have admired the way he handles himself in interviews, refusing to be drawn into any controversies yet offering a constructive and balanced view on the game.

You do not really appreciate how good Alan is until you have played alongside him. He took a lot of pressure off me during my early days in the England team and gave me loads of invaluable advice.

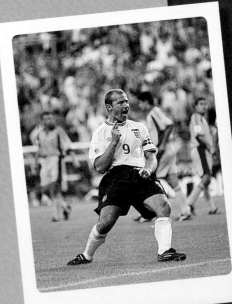

Gianfranco Zola (Chelsea)

' His speed and mobility have become a vital attacking weapon for Chelsea. '

He has got two of the quickest and best feet I have ever seen on a football field. Just as important he has got the brain to go with them. His speed and mobility have become a vital attacking weapon for Chelsea.

The little Italian does a lot of his work out in the wide positions and it is there you realise how skilful he is. He can beat players on either side and it must be a nightmare for defenders to try to pin him down. He also has a great appreciation of what is going on around him and you see him bring players into play who are better positioned rather than go it alone.

Maybe he does not score goals at the same rate these days as earlier in his career, but he is still very dangerous from free kicks anywhere around the penalty area with his ability to swerve and dip a dead ball around defensive walls.

That's not a bad collection, is it? I would back them against anything in the Premiership and certainly wouldn't fancy facing them every week. You will notice that apart from Vieira and Zola, my team is made up of home-grown players. It is not that I have anything against foreign imports because I think the really good ones have done a lot to improve the quality of our league.

There is a constant argument that the influx of overseas players is stifling the development of our own talent but I cannot go along completely with that view. The truly world class stars have had been a good influence particularly in the way they prepare for matches. Where I would draw the line is when clubs bring in cheap imports, especially younger ones, and just have them sitting on the bench. They are standing in the way of the kids who have come through the club ranks and are trying to make their way in the game.

Eventually I am sure there will have to be a restriction on how many foreigners each club can sign. There has to be the right balance between allowing the quality imports into our league and stopping the flood of ordinary players who are no better than the ones who deserve the chance to shine in the Premiership.

FUTURE

So much has happened to me in such a short space of time, I have to pinch myself sometimes to make sure I have not been dreaming it all. However, despite all the high peaks I have reached in my brief professional career, I have never been one to live my life with my head in the clouds.

I appreciate that in football terms I am still a relative newcomer and have such a lot to learn. I know from speaking to my fellow professionals, who have been through much more than me, that you can still be learning about the game when you are 30, let alone when you are 20. I have never been fooled into believing I am the complete player – even when I was being hailed as the greatest thing since sliced bread after returning from France 98.

Just because I have played for a couple of seasons in the Premiership and have taken part in the World Cup finals does not mean I know it all. I am continually analysing my game and seeking ways to improve it. For example, I know I have got to improve my left foot, develop my heading ability and learn to hold the ball up better with my back to goal. I hate defending but around 50 per cent of a game is played when the opposition has the ball so I have got to get better at that as well.

They are aspects of football I cannot hide from if I am going to realise my full potential. They are not what my game is all about because I prefer to be running at the opposition with the ball at my feet. I will continue to utilise those skills but work on my weaknesses as well.

If I look back at my career so far, you will see I have not had what you would call a normal football apprenticeship. I never really spent too much time in the Liverpool youth or reserve teams. I was thrown in at the deep end and within my first season as a Premiership player was called up into the England squad. Not that I am complaining about that. Who wouldn't want to be playing at the highest level at such a young age?

But it has meant I have had to learn my trade at the sharp end of the business and, of course, I have made mistakes along the way. I would not be normal if I had not. It still hurts, though, to read critical newspaper articles. I have never claimed I am the finished article but I would still back my scoring record and performance level against most of the strikers in the country.

I even managed to learn a lot when I was not playing too much football at the end of the 1998-99 and start of the following season. It was a frustrating time for me because I had never been injured before – and that makes a mockery of the suggestions at the time that I am injury prone. But it did take me longer than I expected to shake off the problem and I was able to understand the need for patience and a careful rehabilitation to make sure something like a hamstring strain is fully mended before you attempt a comeback.

I am fortunate to be with Liverpool at a time when they seem to be re-emerging as a real force again and I want to be part of a squad that restores the club to the place it once held at the very top of the football ladder. I suppose I was lucky in a way to have been born and brought up within half an hour's reach of one of the greatest clubs in the world.

" I know I have got to improve my left foot, develop my heading ability and learn to hold the ball up better with my back to goal... "

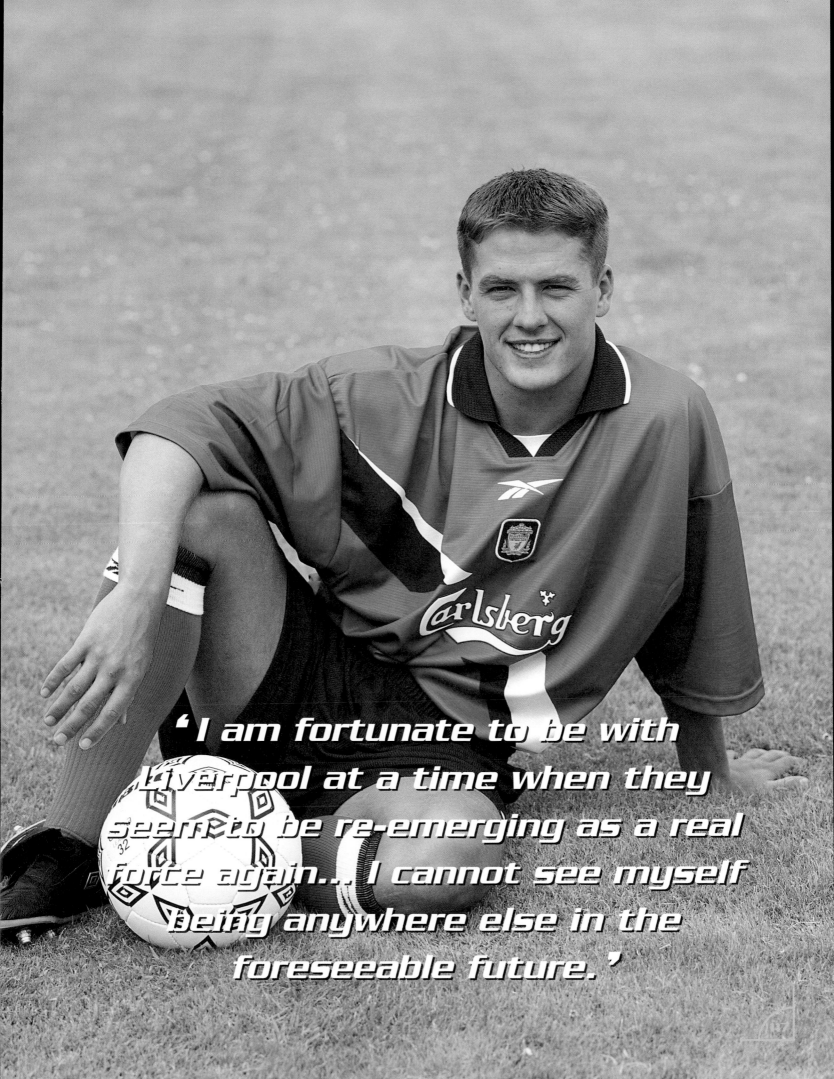

'I am fortunate to be with Liverpool at a time when they seem to be re-emerging as a real force again... I cannot see myself being anywhere else in the foreseeable future.'

I cannot see myself being anywhere else in the foreseeable future. I have signed three contracts with Liverpool – one when I first turned professional, a second during my first full season and a third when I returned from the World Cup. Each time they approached me with their offers, which proved to me how much they valued me.

The last deal I agreed ties me to Anfield until the end of the 2002/3 season and I am happy with that arrangement. My home, my family and my football are all in place and I don't see any reasons to disturb them.

As for the long-term future, well, you cannot afford to look too far into the distance in football. It is very rare, though, for one player to stay at the same club for up to 15 years any more. So perhaps it is unrealistic to think I will spend the whole of my career at Liverpool. We will have to wait and see.

There was a time when I was a starry-eyed youngster that I could see myself playing abroad – probably in Italy– at some stage. All the best players in the world seemed to be there and some of England's top performers such as Paul Gascoigne and David Platt were being tempted over by big money contracts.

I thought of how glamorous it would all be but gradually have started to realise what a big wrench it would mean to leave behind my friends and family to go and live a long way from home and have to learn a new language and way of life. But the bottom line is that I want to play my football in the best league in the world and at the moment the Premiership is on a par with anything else.

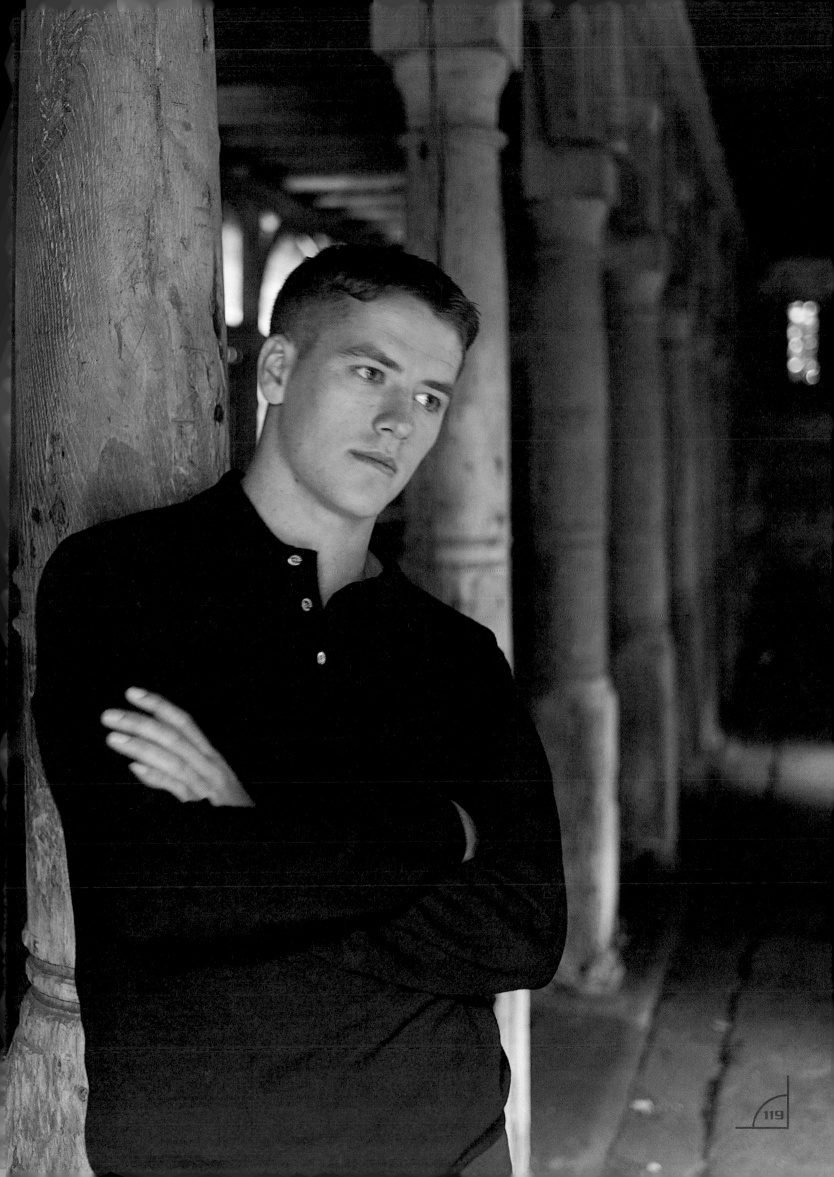

There was speculation in the media about a move to Italy for me at one stage with Lazio ready to pay £25 million, but as far as I was concerned that is all it was – pure speculation.

I am often asked what else is there left for me to achieve having done so much so early in my career. The answer is that in football terms I have not won anything yet. Football is a team game and that means winning the top honours such as Premiership titles, FA Cups, the European Champions League and on the international stage European Championships and World Cups. Those are the real prizes in the game.

While it is fabulous to pick up individual awards and sports personality trophies and to watch endless replays of that goal against Argentina, they don't satisfy all my ambitions as a footballer.

At the end of my career, I want to be able to look in the cabinets in my snooker room and see them full of cups, caps and medals. I have not made a bad start to my life in football and I would not change any of it. Hopefully there are a lot more good things in store for me.

'I have not made a bad start to my life in football and I would not change any of it.'